WALKS
THROUGH
HISTORY

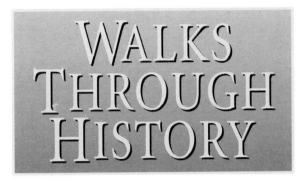

WALKS THROUGH HISTORY

DERBYSHIRE

with
John Wilks

Evening **Telegraph**

Breedon Books
Publishing Company
Derby

First published in Great Britain by
The Breedon Books Publishing Company Limited
Breedon House, 44 Friar Gate, Derby, DE1 1DA.
1999

ISBN 1 85983 166 4

Printed and bound by Butler & Tanner Ltd., Selwood Printing Works,
Caxton Road, Frome, Somerset.

Colour separations by GreenShires Creative Colour Ltd, Leicester.

Jackets printed by Lawrence-Allen Ltd, Avon.

Contents

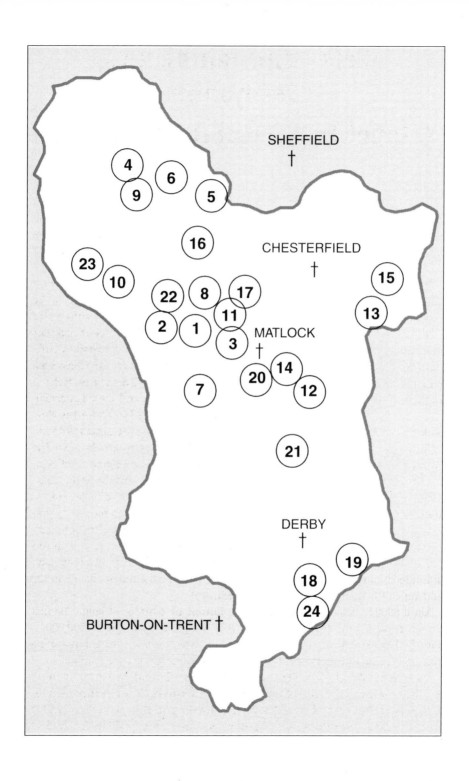

Walks through historic Derbyshire
A brief historical introduction

Each walk in this book has been chosen not only because it is a pleasant walk in its own right, but also because it goes past sites which reveal the rich and varied history of the county. The walks are arranged chronologically, each walk having a major historical theme, and together they take the walker through 12,000 years of Derbyshire's history. The purpose of this introduction is to show how each of the walks in this collection fits into the overall history of the county.

It is often said that Derbyshire is a borderland between northern and southern England. The south of the county is part of the soft agricultural land of the Midlands, whilst the north and west belong to the rugged hill country of northern England. The east of the county, with its collieries and factories, is part of industrial Britain, whilst the west is part of an agricultural landscape little changed for hundreds of years. Historically too, Derbyshire has often been on a border. It marked the original limit of the Roman Empire after their invasion of southern England; it was the border between the Britons and the encroaching Anglo-Saxons, and later between the Anglo-Saxons and the Danes; for the Normans it was a buffer zone between the conquered south and the unsettled north.

Although Derbyshire can be regarded as a border, it was never a frontier. The county has been very self-contained for much of its history, on the edges of great historic convulsions but standing apart from them. In large part this is due to its geographical position at the southern end of the Pennines. The major north-south arteries run either side of the Pennine range, and tend to by-pass Derbyshire. In consequence, although Derbyshire often marked a boundary between opposing cultures, it has not been fought over to the same degree as many other counties. This is not to say that Derbyshire's history is insignificant, and indeed, during the Industrial Revolution, perhaps the major change in the landscape of Britain, the county was pre-eminent.

Until 6000BC Britain was connected to Europe by a bridge of land. The first human beings came to Britain across this bridge as long ago as 500,000BC. Initially they searched for roots and berries, but eventually hunted animals using stone tools. Men during this 'Palaeolithic' or Old Stone Age era were nomadic and very few in number. They built no permanent homes, but camped in the open air, and the only traces they left of their passing were within the caves they used for occasional shelter. One of the oldest human dwellings in Britain is to be found at Cresswell Crags in eastern Derbyshire, where caves were periodically lived in from 50,000BC. After the end of the Ice Age in 10,000BC, the climate gradually improved. Man came in increasing numbers to Derbyshire, still as a nomadic hunter following the herds of animals and the growing season of plants. During this seasonal migration, certain caves such as some in Lathkill Dale (walk 1) were regularly used, for shelter and for religious ceremony.

Man started to settle in Derbyshire from around 4500BC, gradually making the transition from hunter-gatherer to farmer. Forests were managed and crops were planted and cultivated for food. By 3000BC man was living in permanent settlements on the sides of sheltered valleys of the Peak District, where the light soils were easy to cultivate. This became one of most densely habited parts of Britain. The population during this 'Neolithic' or New Stone Age was still small and widely scattered, with only 20,000 people in the whole of the British Isles. Neolithic man lived in wooden huts with no foundations, which left no mark upon the environment. They did however build huge enclosures, or 'henges' of stone and earth, such as Arbor Low (walk 2).

The discovery of how to work metal into tools revolutionised prehistoric society. The Bronze Age in Britain started around 2500BC in the south-east of the country. Improved agricultural techniques led to a rapid expansion in the population. Pressure for land gradually forced Bronze Age settlers, known as Beaker Folk, northwards and westwards. They penetrated Derbyshire up the valleys of the Trent, the Derwent and the Wye, and by 1750BC Bronze Age culture prevailed, spreading higher onto the limestone plateau as the climate improved. These Bronze Age people were farmers, organised into tribes or clans. They lived in circular houses with stone foundations, and buried their dead in round graves or tumuli. The moors above Curbar Edge have extensive remains of Bronze Age fields and houses. On Stanton Moor (walk 3) there are over 70 tumuli inter-spersed with fields. A steadily growing population led to ever greater demand for good agricultural land, and inter-tribal competition became common. The new techniques in metal working were employed to produce weapons. A warrior elite ruled society, and tribes built huge hill forts such as that at Mam Tor (walk 4), for protection but also to display the prestige and status of the builders.

From 1000BC onwards the climate steadily deteriorated, becoming colder and wetter. The uplands were abandoned, and people migrated into the valleys and the plains to the south of the county. Competition for land intensified, made worse by an increasing birthrate. At the same time iron, easier to work and more readily available than bronze, was increasingly used for making tools and weapons. For protection, tribes and clans now coagulated into loose confed-erations and petty kingdoms. As the threat of lawlessness increased, so too did the number and strength of the hill forts such as Carl Wark (walk 5), built now with defence as the primary purpose. Derbyshire became a borderland between the arable lands of the south and the wild hill country of the Pennine moors.

When the Romans invaded Britain in 43AD they found a country divided between many different tribes, some of whom opposed the invaders, many of whom accepted them. The Roman legions landed in Kent, and rapidly swept north and west. They reached lowland Derbyshire in 47AD, and built a fort on the site of modern Derby to control the area. This was the land of the Coritani tribe, who put up no resistance to Rome and were peacefully occupied. By 54AD the Romans controlled all of the land south of a line from the Humber to the Severn, including lowland Derbyshire, and were content for that to be the extent of their new province of Brittania.

The Pennines and the Peak District were within the territory of the largest of all British Iron Age tribes, the Brigantes, who ruled most of northern Britain. Initially, Rome was happy to leave the Brigantes as an independent client kingdom, but in 69AD the Brigantes became hostile, provoking a Roman invasion. The first northward thrusts of the invasion were to either side of the Pennines, but in 78AD the Romans occupied the Peak District, to secure their flanks and to control the lead known to exist in the area. Forts were built at modern-day Glossop and Hope (walk 6) to control the region. Once the area was pacified, a spa developed around the garrison town of Buxton (walk 23). For the next three centuries the Roman lead mines supplied lead throughout the Empire, for coins, water piper, and pewter artefacts. Although Derbyshire did not see the development of the affluent villas which formed the basis of rural life further south, farms owned and worked by romanised Britons prospered in the buoyant economy the romans created (walk 7).

By the fourth century Roman rule in Britain was crumbling. Much of northern Britain was ruled by Picts and Scots, and in the south some Saxons had been allowed to settle in Britain, to provide a buffer against further Saxon encroachment. When the Romans finally withdrew in 410AD, Anglo-Saxon tribes poured into Britain in increasing numbers, through Kent, Sussex and East Anglia. Angles from Denmark gradually pushed up the river valleys to occupy the south of Derbyshire. By 600AD all of England south of a line from the Humber to the Severn was divided into numerous small Anglo-Saxon kingdoms. North and west of that were kingdoms containing a hybrid of Picts, Scots, Saxons and Britons. Derbyshire again became a borderland, this time between the Anglo-Saxon kingdom of Mercia in the south and the Norse kingdom of York to the north. For a time the Peak was a independent kingdom of a people called the Pecsaetes, romanised survivors of the original ancient British inhabitants of the area. This provided a buffer zone, with huge earth embankments to mark the frontiers between Saxon and Norse lands (walk 6). Gradually however, Anglo-Saxons colonised the Peak and eventually it too was incorporated into Mercia.

From 800AD norsemen from Scandinavia started raiding northern and eastern Britain. Raids turned into a permanent occupation known as Danelaw. Norwegian kingdoms were founded in Scotland and Cumbria, and Danish kingdoms in Yorkshire and East Anglia. Danes thrust up the River Trent in 874AD and founded Deoraby (or Derby) as the capital of a kingdom which included all of the lowlands and the White Peak but left the Dark Peak as a buffer between Dane to the south and Norwegian to the north. Further Norse advance into England was halted in 878-9AD by Alfred the Great, king of Wessex. In 914AD his son, Edward the Elder, embarked upon a campaign to unite the disparate Anglo-Saxon kingdoms into one. Over the next six years armies led by Edward and his sister Elfleda, swept north and east out of Wessex, conquering Saxon and Dane alike. Derby was captured in 917AD, and in 920AD Edward captured and fortified Bakewell. Here he called a great 'summit' conference of all the surrounding kingdoms, where borders were ratified and differences settled. Edward was elected overlord of England, the first effective ruler of a united England since the romans had departed (walk 8).

Under Edward's successors, the county map of England as we know it today was created. Derbyshire was created as a separate county around 1000AD. It was the last English county to be created, a reflection of its position on an unimportant border. The strength of Wessex was short-lived, and between 980 and 1016 Britain suffered a further massive influx of Danish. conquerors. Making virtue of necessity, much of Eastern England was given to the Danes. Derbyshire became part of this new Danish kingdom, whose ruler, Canute, eventually became king of all England.

Christianity had been imposed upon Britain in the fourth century ad by Emperor Constantine, but was driven underground when pagan tribes arrived, with their own religion. Christian missionaries had been re-entering Britain from the sixth century onwards. In Derbyshire, these missionaries travelled south from Cumbria, preaching in the open air and reconverting the inhabitants to Christianity. Richly decorated stone crosses were erected on the moors to mark the preaching sites, over thirty of which have been found in Derbyshire (walks 8 and 16).

In 1066 William the Conqueror landed in Sussex and subdued southern England within a matter of months to become King. The Norman conquest was resisted for several more years in northern England. The hill country of Derbyshire and Yorkshire provided sanctuary for guerrilla fighters, and rebellious Anglo-Saxon lords were aided by a Danish army which landed in the Humber. In 1069-70 William sent a considerable army northwards in order to establish his rule. The rebellion was put down with considerable brutality with many executions across northern England. To avoid further rebellion, William gave much of Derbyshire and northern Nottinghamshire to his illegitimate son, William Peveril, as a personal fiefdom, to act as a buffer zone between the pacified south and the unruly north. Peveril oversaw the creation of two huge Royal Forests as private hunting preserves of the crown, one along the Derwent valley around Duffield, the second on the High Peak. Peveril many powerful castles with which to control his lands, at Castleton (walk 9) and at Duffield, others at Bolsover, Mackworth and Codnor.

Norman feudalism was rigorously imposed upon southern England, but was not introduced into Derbyshire to the same extent. However, the peasantry in Derbyshire shared the same farming practices as existed further south, based upon communal fields around a central village (walk 10). From the twelfth century onwards, under the encouragement of the Crown, the English textile trade expanded dramatically, bringing with it a greatly increased demand for wool. To meet this, agricultural activity changed and increased. Land was enclosed, creating large fields suitable for sheep-grazing. Monasteries in southern England were given huge grants of land in the hill country of Derbyshire, upon which to raise sheep. These monastic farms or 'granges' drastically altered the appearance of the landscape (walks 1, 2 and 7)

With its subjugation by the Normans, Derbyshire slipped out of the mainstream of English history. It was neither a rich county, nor a vital frontier, and did not stand upon important routes to anywhere. Until the mid-sixteenth century the county affairs of Derbyshire, such as law enforcement and tax collection, were administered from Nottingham. Much of its land was administered by the Duchy of Lancaster. Before 1566 it did not even have its own shire court. Many of Derbyshire's great land-owning families were content to attend to affairs within their own county and to avoid involvement in national politics. Typical of this were the Manners and Vernon families, landowners in Derbyshire from 1139, whose home was at Haddon Hall (walk 11). For other great landowners, Derbyshire provided a country retreat. Lord Cromwell, Chancellor to Henry VI and one of the most powerful men in the England of his day, built a palace at Wingfield on the edge of the forest of Duffield Frith, where he could escape from affairs of state and relax (walk 12).

Few of the properties owned by religious orders in Derbyshire survived the Dissolution of the Monasteries, ordered by Henry VIII in the years 1535-40. Local gentry such as Sir William Cavendish were appointed as commissioners to oversee the dissolution, and they had ample opportunity to profit from their task. Cavendish was able to greatly enhance his lands and fortune through the purchase of such church properties as Buxton (walk 23) and Calke Abbey (walk 24). Cavendish married Bess of Hardwick, one of the most controversial women in Elizabeth I's court (walk 13) and founded one of Derbyshire's leading dynasties. After the death of Cavendish, Bess went on to marry the Earl of Shrewsbury, who had vast estates in Derbyshire. It was in part these estates that led to Shrewsbury's appointment as gaoler to Mary, Queen of Scots, who had fled to England in 1568, and for the next seventeen years was under house arrest. Shrewsbury's Derbyshire properties were chosen partly because of their remoteness from the centre of English political life. Mary spent periods at Sheffield Castle, Chatsworth House (walk 17) and Wingfield Manor (walk 12), and it was whilst she was at the latter that a young Derbyshire gentleman named Anthony Babington devised his ill-conceived plot to free Mary (walk 14).

At the start of the Civil War in 1642 Derbyshire was one of the smallest and poorest counties in England, with a population of only 68,000. It largely escaped the ravages of that conflict. There was little actual fighting within the county, and comparatively few of the population saw the necessity of joining either side. Wingfield Manor was besieged, and Bolsover Castle (walk 15) was ruined after the War. Bolsover was home to a later William Cavendish, Earl of Newcastle, who had come to prominence under the early Stuart kings and had made Bolsover the finest Palladian mansion in England. He had command of the Royalist forces in the north from 1642-4, but fled into exile after the battle of Marston Moor.

Derbyshire was not so lucky in escaping the ravages of the Great Plague, that swept through England in 1665-6, and killed up to 10% of the population. The county suffered far less than it might thanks to the self sacrifice of the tiny village of Eyam (walk 16). When plague broke out in the village, its inhabitants chose to quarantine themselves rather than risk spreading the decease across the county. Three quarters of the villagers lost their lives in consequence.

The Cavendish family played a major part in another great drama of the Stuart Era. The 4th Earl of Devonshire was one of the noblemen who invited William of Orange, later William III, to come to England and depose his father-in-law James II in what has become known as the Glorious Revolution (walk 17). When William landed at Torbay in 1688, Cavendish raised an armed force on his Chatsworth Estates and marched to seize the strategically important Nottingham for the rebels. Derbyshire also witnessed the final end of Stuart hopes sixty years later. In 1745 Bonnie Prince Charlie led a victorious Scottish army into England, marching on London to overthrow the Hanoverian dynasty. The Prince reached Derby before his generals refused to go any further (walk 18), and turned around to retreat to Scotland and eventual defeat.

By the middle of the eighteenth century most of the elements necessary for the great upsurge in manufacturing known as the Industrial Revolution were available. Still missing was the means to move large volumes of raw materials and finished goods around the country quickly and cheaply. Roads were unsurfaced and of poor quality, and rivers were un-navigable for any distance. In Derbyshire as elsewhere, the transport of goods relied upon carts or, in hill country, packhorses. Turnpike roads had made passenger transport easier, but they were not suitable for the bulk movement of freight. The situation was revolutionised in 1761, when the Duke of Bridgewater opened the first commercial canal in England. Over the next sixty years 'canal-mania' swept Britain. A network of canals soon connected Derbyshire with the rest of the country. The Grand Trunk Canal, linking the Rivers Humber and Mersey, passed close to Derby, and a network of spur canals and inland ports (walk 19) grew up connecting the rest of the county with this major artery of trade.

The development of canals removed the final obstacle to the explosion of industrial development. If Derbyshire had been on the periphery of English history since the Norman conquest, it now came to centre stage. The early Industrial Revolution relied upon water to drive its new machines, and the plentiful fast flowing rivers of Derbyshire were an ideal source for this. Richard Arkwright became the first man to apply water power to driving machinery, at his textile mill in Cromford (walk 20). New machinery required new buildings or factories to house them, and a plentiful supply of cheap labour, which needed to be housed near the workplace. The factory and the industrial town, the hallmark of industrial development throughout the modern world, came into being in Derbyshire, which can rightly claim the title 'the Cradle of the Industrial Revolution'. Some of these new industrial towns, like Cromford, grew from virtually nothing: others, like Belper (walk 21), were developed upon an existing village, whose existing cottage industry provided the nucleus for the new town.

So fast was the pace of change once the Industrial Revolution was underway that within sixty years industry and transport moved away from water as a source of power. The canal was superseded by the railway as a means of transport, and railways rapidly spread across Derbyshire from 1831 onwards. The first steam railways used static engines to pull trucks up inclines and thereafter used horse power to pull them (walk 20). With the invention of the steam locomotive, railways spread rapidly, although their progress across the huge estates of the landed gentry was often contested (walks 11 and 17.) Steam-driven machines also replaced water-driven ones in the factories. The growth of steam power, both in factories and for transport, greatly increased the need for coal. Coal made been mined in Derbyshire on a relatively small scale since Elizabethan days (walk 15), but the hugely increased demand led to the development of the coal fields in the east of the county. Factories were no longer confined to banks of rivers for their power source, and new factories sprang up conveniently near the coalmines that supplied their energy needs. Gradually the focus of industry shifted way from central Derbyshire to the east and to the coalfields of Yorkshire.

Ironically, if the abundance of water in Derbyshire led to the explosion of new industries, it was the death of the county's oldest industry. Lead had been mined in Derbyshire since the Iron Age, and reached its peak between 1700 and 1750. Even during the early years of the industrial revolution, lead mining was still the largest and most profitable industry in the county, apart from agriculture (walk 22). However, as the demand for lead increased, ever deeper mines were needed, which dug down to the water table and flooded. Many ingenious engineering feats were undertaken to keep the pits dry enough to be worked, but ultimately to no avail. Lead mining became too unprofitable to be worthwhile and by the end of the nineteenth century the industry was effectively dead (walks 1 and 22).

Even before the Industrial Revolution in Derbyshire had reached its peak, the foundations were being laid for a new and enduring industry, tourism. The 5th Duke of Devonshire realised the potential of Buxton as a spa town as early as 1780, and started developing facilities for wealthy visitors. In the early nineteenth century the 6th Duke created an infrastructure to enable the town to capitalise upon the growing Victorian passion for tourism (walk 23). Improved communications in the nineteenth century meant that Derbyshire was no longer a remote backwater but was within easy reach of the rest of the country. Tourism continued to develop throughout the nineteenth and twentieth centuries. In 1951 the Peak District became Britain's first National Park, and tourism has remained an important part of the county's economy up until the present.

Derbyshire remained however a tranquil county, and was a haven of relaxation for the wealthy and powerful as well as a tourist destination. Two of Queen Victoria's prime ministers, Melbourne and Palmerston, both made Derbyshire into a retreat from the rigours of Parliament (walk 24). Even today, when travel is ever faster and easier, the centre and north of the county still feels remarkably remote and isolated, and to enter the Peak National Park is to step back in time. In many ways Derbyshire remains as it has been through much of its history, a border between two worlds.

Advice to Walkers

All of the walks in this collection are across open countryside for at least part of their route. Although the terrain is not difficult or dangerous, it can become very wet and slippery in places, especially after a shower of rain, and walking boots or stout shoes are recommended for any of these walks. It is also recommended that you carry waterproofs, since the weather can change quickly in Derbyshire, and you could easily find yourself some distance away from shelter when the skies open. Remember that on some walks there may be occasional brambles, nettles or crops which scratch, so bear this in mind when deciding whether to walk in shorts.

Directions for each walk are given in the text and a sketch map included to give an outline of the route. These sketch maps are not detailed enough to navigate by, and it is strongly recommended that you carry the relevant Ordnance Survey map, in case of difficulties or in case you wish to deviate from the route. The 1:50,000 series is perfectly adequate to walk from. Although all directions are accurate at the time of writing, features do occasionally change: a hedge or tree may disappear, a stile may be replaced by a gate. By comparing the written directions with the OS map it should be perfectly possible to find the correct route even if features have occasionally altered.

All routes in this book use public rights of way or permissive footpaths when crossing private land. Again, the OS map will confirm the right of way in case of doubt. If a footpath or bridleway is shown on a current map, it is the duty of the landowner to maintain the route and you have a legal right to use it. However, it is sensible to show discretion and compromise rather than a rigid insistence on your rights: for instance, if at certain times of the year the route across an open field is not obvious or is obscured by crops, it may be better to walk around the perimeter of the field.

Consideration for others is key when walking, and at all times remember the Countryside Code laid down by the Countryside Commission:

1. **Enjoy the countryside and respect its life and work.**
2. **Guard against all risk of fire**
3. **Fasten all gates.**
4. **Keep your dogs under close control**
5. **Keep to public paths across farmland**
6. **Use gates and stiles to cross fences, hedges and walls**
7. **Leave livestock, crops and machinery alone.**
8. **Take your litter home**
9. **Help to keep all water clean.**
10. **Protect wildlife, plants and trees**
11. **Take special care on country roads**
12. **Make no unnecessary noise**

I have indicated where refreshments can be obtained on each walk. On a number of the walks, refreshments are only available at the beginning or end. It is therefore advisable to carry a snack, and more importantly something to drink with you, especially on the longer walks. Please note that the mention of the existence of a pub is not necessarily an endorsement of it!

Convenient car parking places have been indicated for all walks. At the time of writing, many of these were free and there is adequate parking at most spots indicated. Should you have difficulty it is far better to find a different parking spot and make your way to the start of the walk on foot, rather than causing an obstruction with your car. Most importantly, remember you are visiting a place where other people live. Do not cause inconvenience to local people by parking across access to houses, farms, fields or churches.

Walk 1

Lathkill Dale: the arrival of Man

Distance: 7 miles

Map: OS sheet 119

Start and parking: The walk starts from the pay & display car park in the village of Over Haddon (grid ref: 202664). Over Haddon is on a minor road, south of the B5055 Bakewell to Monyash road, and is two miles south from Bakewell itself.

Refreshments: Public House and café at craft centre in Over Haddon, also seasonal tearooms.

Historical Background

The last great Ice Age lasted for a million years and ended 10,000 years ago. At its height, vast glaciers extended from the polar ice caps as far south as the Peak District. The name 'Ice Age' is misleading, for there were many climatic fluctuations, ranging from bitterly cold phases when the glaciers advanced, interspersed with warm, sometimes sub-tropical phases. These phases lasted for tens of thousands of years, and in the warm interludes the region of present-day Derbyshire was grazed by elephant, rhinoceros and hippopotamus. These animals were hunted by the first men, who visited Derbyshire 500,000 years ago. This Ice Age period is known as the Palaeolithic, or 'Old Stone Age', and during this period early humans were hunter-gatherers. They collected roots and tubers, nuts and berries, and used primitive weapons to hunt animals, for food and for their hides and antlers. Normally they lived in the open, under the sky or in crude temporary grass shelters, using caves upon occasions. They travelled huge distances each year in a systematic search for food. They came in very small numbers, and left little mark upon the landscape, but traces of their passing have been found in caves throughout Derbyshire. One such site is Lathkill Dale.

The glaciers started their last, gradual retreat 10,000 years ago, leaving behind them a barren landscape. In the valleys and on the plains south of the Peak there were stunted trees, and low-lying sedge grasses; on the millstone uplands there was a tundra-like landscape of bleak exposed rocks and beds of moss. For the next 5000 years, known as the Mesolithic or 'Middle Stone Age', the climate gradually improved, becoming warmer and moister, with forests replacing the tundra. Man continued to be a hunter-gatherer, but by now his tools were more sophisticated, dogs were domesticated and used for hunting, and he lived in more sturdy wooden huts. The numbers of men in Derbyshire were very small, only a hundred or so across the whole county, living in small family groups. Their life-style was still nomadic, but they moved on a regular, carefully planned, seasonal round. They followed the herds of game, moving onto the upland plateaux in summer in search of fruits, returning to sheltered valleys for the winter. The heavily forested plains of southern Derbyshire were avoided, and the favoured habitation during this Mesolithic period was the Peak.

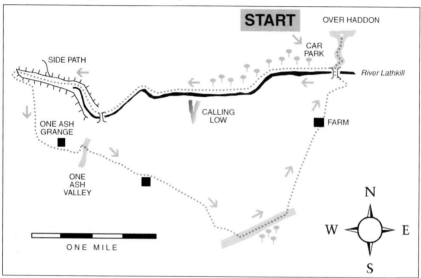

The Walk

This walk goes along the rugged Lathkill Dale, passing near to prehistoric cave dwellings, and returns across the plateau through open fields. The first part of the walk is on a permissive path.

- Leave the car park by the exit beside the toilet block. Facing the Yew Tree Tea Rooms, turn right down the lane, soon passing St Anne's church.
- At the bottom of the hill, DO NOT go down to the river but keep right through a wooden gate and pass beside a building to a second gate 20 yards later.
- Go through the gate and along the permissive footpath, the river on your left. (The landowners reserve the right to close this path, although in practice this is extremely rare.)

18

● Keep along the river bank. In 500 yards note a disused mineshaft on your
   right, and a manmade channel in the river, known as a 'sough', on your left.

*Lead mining was an important industry in the Peak District since the Iron Age.
Many of the mines were initially shallow excavations in the sides of dales, where the
steeply eroded valleys had exposed the mineral seams. Over the years the mines
gradually increased in depth but as they were dug deeper flooding was increasingly
a problem. The first answer was to build a 'sough', a drainage channel to allow water
to pour by gravity out of the mine into a nearby river (see walk 22). By 1803 the
Alport field here in Lathkill was using Richard Trevithick's newly invented water
pressure engine to pump water out of deeper mines. Steam engines were later used
for the same purpose, but to no avail: the mines kept flooding, making the extraction
of deep lead uneconomic. In 1851 the Mandale Mining Co. ceased trading, followed
the next year by Lathkill's other mining company, Alport mines.*

*The closure of the mines cost jobs and profits, and Lathkill faced economic ruin.
However, two years later deposits of toadstone, believed to be gold bearing, were
found in Lathkill. The Over Haddon Gold & Silver Mining Company was floated,
with shares in the company briefly in high demand. Further assessment however
revealed that there was no gold in Lathkill and the company collapsed. Whether the
initial find was wishful thinking, a result of the 'gold fever' which followed recent
finds in California and Australia, or was a deliberate confidence trick, has never been
proved. Either way, mining in Lathkill ceased after 1856.*

● Keep along the river bank for another mile, passing a weir, and 100 yards later
   go through a squeeze stile leading out of the Lathkill Dale Nature Reserve.

*Look to your left, across the river. The steep sided wooded valley opposite is Calling
Low. Traces of early man have been found in caves in that valley. A number of flint
tools have been found, very sophisticated in their design, with barbed arrowheads
and specialised hand tools, some designed for cutting, some for scraping, some for
chopping.*

*When the ice caps melted, the seas rose and the landbridge between Britain and
Europe was eventually submerged, making Britain an island for the first time 6000
years ago. One result was that fertile coastal plains rich in wildlife were now under
the sea, reducing the hunting area available. Man no longer moved as far in his
forage for food, but tended to be based more on a specific area. The warmer climate
had resulted in a greater forest cover, and this part of Lathkill would have looked
much as it does today. Man used this valley and the side valleys leading off it for his
winter habitation, for it was sheltered from the winter winds by the steep sided
valley, with a plentiful supply of good quality water. In the spring he moved up onto
the plateau above, following the herds of deer that provided food and raw materials,
and searching for edible summer fruits and roots, before returning to the valleys in
the autumn.*

Stone Age men were not cave dwellers: for most of the year they constructed their homes, either grass and wood huts for the winter months or skin tents to be carried on their summer food forays. But caves were used, either as temporary shelter for hunters caught away from home, or for ceremonial purposes. The sites of such caves were carefully noted and the knowledge down through the generations. The caves in Calling Low were regularly used as temporary shelters over a period of many centuries.

● Continue ahead through less wooded scenery, following the footpath with the river on your left.

● After threequarters of a mile, ignore a footbridge and continue upstream.

● After a further half a mile you come to the point where the stream emerges from a limestone cave. Continue ahead up the increasingly narrow valley.

The frost-shattered crags in the valley here clearly show the results of the Ice Age. Huge rivers of thawing glacial water flooded down the narrow valleys, cutting deep trenches through the plateau and exposing the limestone to the effects of rain and frost. This erosion created caves such as those seen up on the right, and caves such as these attracted man to Lathkill. They provided nomadic hunters with immediately available shelter from the elements.

● Go through a squeeze stile. Ignore a path just beyond that climbs the steep slope to the right via steps, but instead continue ahead up the gorge-like valley for a further quarter of a mile. The path initially clambers through rocks, and then levels out.

● At the top of the valley go through a kissing gate into a field. Ignore the gate ahead, but go forward 20 yards, and then turn sharp left, over steps in the wall beside a gate on your left.

● Follow a green track uphill, a wall on your left hand and Lathkill Dale now down below you on the left. Follow the track as it curves right at the field corner, to a metal field gate.

● Go through the gate and keep ahead along the track, the wall on your left hand.

● At the end of the field follow the track through a gateway and keep straight on across the next field, to a field gate.

● Go through the gate and turn left down an enclosed track towards a farm.

This is One Ash Grange Farm, and its name reflects its mediaeval origin. In the middle of the twelfth century Henry II recognised the potential that the almost uninhabited lands of the Peak offered for raising sheep, whose wool was vital for the growing English textile industry. Monasteries in the south of England were granted vast areas of land in Derbyshire, provided that they established sheep farms. Monastic farms, or 'granges', were built, occupied by lay-brothers under the control of an occasional monk, who raised flocks of sheep in huge fields. Often the local peasants would be evicted to make room for the grange, with was farmed with *ruthless efficiency. One Ash Grange was founded by Roche Abbey, in Yorkshire. The word 'Grange' associated with a farm in the Peaks invariably betrays its monastic origins.*

- Pass a cow shed on your right. Do not turn up a footpath signed 'Cales Farm' but keep straight on into the farm yard.
- Once in the farm yard, immediately bear left, passing between farm buildings. Follow a track to pass between a metal Dutch barn on your left and a stone outbuilding on your right.
- Go through a squeeze stile and down steps into a field. Keep ahead down a grassy valley, with walls on your right.
- Go through a squeeze stile and go down a steep rocky path, soon with a rock face on your left hand.
- At the end of the rock face, turn right at a footpath sign and descend to a stile.
- Cross the stile and climb up the steps opposite, to a kissing gate at the top of the slope.

Pause at the top of the slope and look back into the steep-sided One Ash Valley. In the valley up to the left there is a cave, which was used as a shelter by the very first humans to come into Derbyshire. In this cave were found some blades made out of flint, used as a cutting implement rather like a knife or dagger, and also some reindeer bones that had designs carved into them. These carvings must have taken many hours of labour, carefully whittling the hard bone with stone tools, and served no practical mundane purpose: they were carved either for a religious significance or purely as an artistic expression, over 10,000 years ago.

Caves in Lathkill Dale.

- Go through the kissing gate and keep straight on to the opposite side of the field, to another kissing gate.

- Maintain your line of advance across the next two fields, aiming for a farm seen ahead.

- At the far side of the second field, go through a kissing gate and turn left up the field, with the wall on your left hand, to a kissing gate leading into trees.

- Keep ahead through the band of trees into a paddock.

- Keep straight on across the paddock to a kissing gate, leading onto a path through trees and into a field.

- Turn right down the side of the field to a kissing gate into another field.

- Go half-left across this field, aiming for a step stile in the far corner.

- Cross this stile and go along the side of a field, with the wall on your left hand, to a stile.

- Maintain your line of advance across the next field, to a stile.

- Go half-right across the next very large field, to eventually reach a ladder stile.

- Cross this stile and go half-left across the next two fields, to reach a road.

- Turn left along the road, soon descending past trees. 300 yards past the end of the trees, look for a footpath crossing the road, and cross a ladder stile on your left.

- Go half-right down a large field, aiming for Over Haddon seen ahead.

- Leave the field by a ladder stile and maintain your line of advance across the next two fields to a ladder stile.

- Drop down the next field, still maintaining your line of advance, aiming towards a farm seen ahead. Pass just to the right of a wall seen ahead, and following the wall, continue down the field to a gateway.

- Go through the gateway and down to a ladder stile, just to the right of metal gates.

- Cross farmyard and go between the buildings opposite, at a sign to 'Over Haddon'.

- Pass between cattle pens and through a metal gate into a field.

- Maintain your line of advance across the field. Soon a footpath sign beside a gate comes into view.

- Go through the gate and down a track, which zigzags to the river. Cross the footbridge.

The footbridge was originally a 'clapper bridge', constructed by shaped boulders being placed on the bed of the river and flat stones laid across them to provide passage. These serviceable bridges were constructed in prehistoric times, and it is a tribute to the quality of their design that many still stand today.

- Climb up the lane opposite back to the car park.

Walk 2

Arbor Low, Derbyshire's Stonehenge

Distance: 9 miles

Map: OS sheet 119

Start and parking: The walk starts from the free car park opposite the Methodist Chapel in Monyash (grid ref: 150666) Monyash is on the B5055 seven miles west of Bakewell and ten miles south of Buxton.

Refreshments: Public house, shop and café in Monyash; café and shop at Parsley Hay, two public houses on first part of route.

Historical Background

Human beings had started to manage their environment from at least 4500BC. They planted and harvested crops, especially cereals, rather than relying upon finding them in the wild, and bred animals for food. By 3000BC, the start of the 'Late Stone Age' or Neolithic Era, man had largely ceased his previous nomadic existence and was becoming more settled. Some woodlands were cleared, to provide arable land and also to create clearings, where sweet new shoots would grow and attract wild game, thereby making hunting easier. Other woodland was managed, with trees being coppiced for their timber. There was still a seasonal round to his life in some degree, moving with his animals onto the higher pastures for summer grazing and for hunting, and returning to the sheltered valleys for winter. But man now had permanent timber homes, in the middle of extensive fields surrounded by earthen banks.

Mans permanent habitations in Derbyshire were confined to the limestone plateau, avoiding the exposed gritstone above and the densely forested valleys below. Settlers were also attracted by the light, rich soils of the plateau were easy to work.The population was still very small. There were no more than 20,000 human beings in the whole of the British Isles in 3000BC, and the population on the White Peak was a few hundreds at most. Man still lived in family groups, each family working their own territory and widely separated from their neighbours. These isolated groups regularly met with other groups. Sometimes this was for trade, which even in the Stone Age was extensive, with some trade goods such as stone tools and pottery coming across huge distances. Sometimes the meeting was for religious ceremonies, which took place in massive enclosures known as 'Henges' that were built by multi-community labour and served the population of a whole locality. One such henge is Arbor Low.

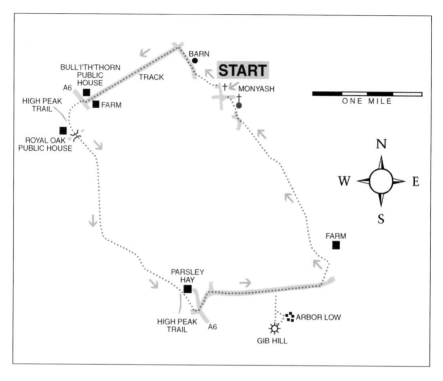

The Walk

This walk goes across the limestone plateau and along part of the High Peaks Trail to visit the ancient henge of Arbor Low. In Derbyshire the word 'Low' as a place-name often means a burial mound on a hill or high place.

- Cross the stile at the back of the car park.
- Turn right and follow the wall on your right hand to a stile into a lane.
- Turn left along the lane for 5 yards and then turn right around the end of the last cottage into an enclosed footpath. Follow the footpath to a stile into a field.

The next part of the route crosses a number of tiny fields, 6 in all, a survival of the medieval field system that surrounded Monyash. The directions for this part take you across 6 fields in 400 yards:

- Cross the stile and turn left along the first field.

24

- Pass through a gap in the wall by a tree and continue your line of advance along the second field to a stile leading into a narrow green lane.

- Cross the green lane to a second stile, then continue your line of advance across the narrow third field to a stile.

- Climb over the stile and continue your line of advance over field four to a squeeze stile.

- Go through the stile and maintain your line of advance across the corner of the next, fifth, field, to a stile beside a telegraph pole.

- Maintain the same line of advance across the sixth and last field to a stile into a lane.

- Turn right along the lane, and then curve left with the lane. Keep ahead along the lane, passing a barn on your right hand.

- Follow the lane for 500 yards to a cross track, 20 yards before a disused cattle shed. Turn right down an enclosed track.

- Follow the enclosed track, with gentle climbs, for a mile.

Looking back from this track you can see a mass of little, stone-walled fields surrounding Monyash. In the thirteenth century the Peak District was a harsh and exposed border region. It had seen a drastic decline in population over the previous two centuries, partly due to a worsening climate driving farmers to lower and more sheltered lands, and partly due to repression following the Norman Conquest (see walk 9). Existing villages were allowed to expand with little restriction, enabling yeoman farmers to recolonise the area. Monyash had two huge open fields around it, and each villager had a number of strips within those fields for his own personal use. Over time, those strips became enclosed by walls, resulting in these tiny fields that have survived unaltered from those mediaeval days. Later on we will see the larger fields of the monastic granges.

- After a mile pass a farm on your left to reach the main A515, next to the Bull'i'th'Thorn public house.

- Cross the road half-right to a stile by a metal field gate.

- Cross the stile and keep straight on across the field to a footpath post and stile.

- Keep straight on down the next field, to another footpath post and stile opposite.

- Cross the stile and go half-left down the next field, going around the shoulder of the hill and down to a gap in the wall.

- Go through the gap and then a quarter-right across the next field, aiming for the arch of a disused railway, seen ahead.

- At the railway arch, do not cross the stile to go under the arch but turn left through the kissing gate by the 'High Peak Trail' sign.

● Follow an enclosed footpath, to climb the embankment onto the High Peak Trail.

This was the route of the Cromford and High Peak Railway (see walk 20), built in 1831 to connect the Peak Forest Canal with the Cromford Canal. It ran for 33 miles through the High Peak, and was initially built to transport limestone from the interior of the White Peak to the canal just south of Cromford, and hence to the rest of England.

● Turn left along the trail, shortly passing under a bridge and passing a house on your right to a gate, leading into the Hurdlow picnic and parking area.

The Royal Oak public house is signposted, a few yards from here.

● Keep straight on along the High Peak Trail, soon leaving the parking/picnic area and continuing along a narrower footpath/cycle track.

● Go along the High Peak Trail for two miles to reach Parsley Hay picnic area.

To the right of the footpath the stone walls of large fields will be seen at intervals. In the fourteenth century many monasteries in the south of England were given vast areas of land on the remote and inhospitable Peak. They established monastic farms or 'Granges' as headquarters for their agriculture, primarily the production of wool. Often the local peasantry were evicted to make room for these farms, which were worked with ruthless efficiency. The Cistercian Abbey of Merevale in Warwickshire was given 250 acres of land here and founded Cronkstone Grange, to which these fields originally belonged. Compare the size of these fields, designed to pasture sheep by land-rich monks, with the tiny domestic fields seen around Monyash.

● Leave the High Peak Trail at Parsley Hay. Pass the café and toilet block on your left hand and continue ahead through the car park and down the drive to a road.

● At the road turn left for 30 yards to reach the main A515.

● Cross the A515 and turn left for 20 yards, then turn right into a side road, signed 'Monyash, Youlgreave, Arbor Low'.

● In 200 yards turn right along a minor road, signed 'Youlgreave' and 'Arbor Low'.

● Continue along this quiet lane for 1200 yards, with views down to the left, into the head of Lathkill Dale.

This area had a rich congregation of farms in the Neolithic era. Each farm was worked by one extended family, well separated from its neighbours. They lived in wooden huts with no stone footings, that therefore left no trace on the landscape. Had you stood here 5,000 years ago and looked down towards Lathkill you would have seen a much gentler landscape than today, one of grassland and open woodland, with extensive fields surrounded by earth banks, and doted with circular houses. The area was settled from about 3000BC onwards, and reached its peak around 2000-1500BC. Although this area was populous by Neolithic standards, only a few families would have lived here.

Arbor Low.

● Turn right at an English Heritage 'Arbor Low' sign and go up a drive. **Access to Arbor Low is on permissive paths across private land. There is a small admission charge for using the paths.**

● Go through the farmyard to two farm gates. Cross a stile to the left of the gates and then turn left up the side of the field, keeping the wall on your left hand.

● Cross a stile. Arbor Low is ahead.

To Stone Age man, 'religious' activity was a part of everyday life. All places were imbued with spirit, and most everyday activities had a ceremonial aspect. The spirits of the dead remained in the world, and played an active role in guiding the living. Some places however had particular religious significance, and monuments were built there for ceremonial purposes. These monuments were associated with special activities, where the living could participate in ceremonies with the dead. They served a whole region, and were built to house many communities upon important occasions. The monuments were surrounded by banks, not for defence but to mark them off from everyday life, and to protect everyday life from the supernatural.

The monuments often had a dual purpose. They were used for 'rites of passage' ceremonies such as birth, puberty, marriage and death, which would take place in front of the whole living community and in the presence of the spirits of the dead. They were also associated with ceremonies marking the natural transformation of the seasons, which were to be celebrated and feared. These ceremonies had the result of bringing together scattered families on a regular basis, where news and goods could be traded, marriages arranged, and tribal identity reinforced.

Arbor Low was constructed around 2500BC and is a superb example of a 'henge', a ceremonial monument surrounded by a circular bank and an earthen ditch. The bank is 8-10 metres wide, 2 metres high, and 75 metres in diameter, surrounded by a ditch 10 metres wide and originally 3 metres deep, dug into rock. All this would have been constructed using simple tools made of bone and antler. It would have taken many years to complete, and must have involved the co-operative labours of people from all the communities in the region.

Within the henge is a circle of 50 or so large limestone slabs. Whether these originally stood upright and have subsequently fallen over, or whether they have always been laid flat, is a matter of conjecture. In the very centre of the circle are two massive slabs, all that remains of a 'cove', a rectangular structure designed to hide ceremonies from view.

There are two entrances through the bank and ditch, one 9 metres wide on the north-west side (the side you have approached from), and a second smaller one to the south-east, which once had a stone gateway and led out into an area of burial mounds.

How the henge was used is unknown, but we can guess that upon special occasions people came from all over the area and gathered within the circle of stones to witness ceremonies performed within the cove by special members of the community. It can be conjectured that the wider entrance was to allow access to the assembled peoples, with the smaller used for ceremonial procession by more limited numbers.

On the southern side of the henge, near the smaller exit, a later, Bronze Age, burial mound has been built onto the side of the embankment.

- To visit Gib Hill, leave the smaller entrance of Arbor Low and turn half-right across the field to a stile in the wall, in direct line with Gib Hill, the mound seen 200 yards away.

- Cross the next field to Gib Hill.

Gib Hill is in reality two barrows, or burial mounds, built one on top of the other. The original barrow is a long barrow, a rectangular earthen mound built over a stone-lined tomb. It was constructed around 3000BC in the Neolithic or 'Stone Age' era, and predates Arbor Low by 1000 years. At that time man lived in social groups based around an extended family, a family that included the dead as well as the living. It is believed that prehistoric man practised some form of ancestor worship or at least reveration. The dead were always present, and provided an on-going link between the present and the past. The tomb would have housed the dead of many generations from the same community, reopened and sealed many times over the centuries. The tomb was built on a conspicuous site for both religious reasons and for territorial ones, the visual presence of the tomb announcing the long-term inter-connection between a people and a specific area of land.

A second tomb was built on top of the long barrow, around 2000BC. this was a round barrow from the Bronze Age, constructed at the same time as the round barrow was built onto the embankment at Arbor Low. By the Bronze Age there was a greatly increased greater pressure upon land and resources, and man was becoming less community minded and more concerned with the status of the individual and his immediate family. Smaller barrows were now built, round in shape, which housed the dead of one family only.

- After viewing Gib Hill, leave the site not by the stile by which you entered, opposite Arbor Low, but by one in the fence at right angles to it, 20 yards to the left of a wooden gate.

- Cross the stile and keep straight on across the field, joining a wall on your left hand. Follow the wall back to the farm and hence to the road.

- Return to the road and turn right. Go along the road for 700 yards. Where the road starts to bend left, with trees lining it on both sides, look out for a footpath post on the left, signed 'Lathkill Dale'.

- Cross the stile and go half-right across the field, aiming for the farmhouse seen ahead.

- Go through a gate and maintain your line of advance across the next field, still aiming at the farmhouse.

- Join a track by a gate. DO NOT go through the gate but turn left up the wall, with the wall on your right hand.

On the left you pass a small, inconspicuous mound. This is a tumulus or burial mound dating from Neolithic times. It would have been from the same era as the original barrow on Gibs Hill. The area you are now walking through would have been land cleared for agricultural use in the Stone Age, an area of large fields interspersed with houses. The tombs of the dead would also have been amongst the fields, for the dead were seen as part of the community and stone age man saw nothing incongruous about sharing his fields with the bodies of his ancestors.

The massive inter-communal henge of Arbor Low is clearly visible on the skyline to the left, and would have dominated the landscape in Neolithic times also.

- Cross a stile at the end of the field and keep ahead, still with the wall on your right hand, to cross a valley and climb up to a stile in the right hand corner ahead.

- Cross the stile and keep straight on up the slope, to a stile in the wall on the far side.

- Keep ahead across the next field, to a stile in the angle of walls opposite.

- Cross the stile and go diagonally across the next field, downhill to a stile in the opposite corner.

- Cross this stile and go half-left across the corner of a field, veering away from the left-hand wall, to a waymark sign.

- Cross the wall and keep half-right along the same line of advance, aiming for a stile on the far side of the field, approximately halfway along the boundary wall.

- Cross the stile and maintain your line of advance across the next field, aiming for the skyline. Once across the skyline, a waymark post becomes visible ahead.

- Go through a gap in the wall and then half-right down the next field, to a squeeze stile in the bottom right-hand corner of the field.

- Go through the squeeze stile and keep ahead on an obvious track across the next field.

- Cross a stile and enter a field at a 'NT Fern Dale' sign. Turn left and follow the wall for 30 yards to a stile by a farm gate.

- Cross the stile into an enclosed footpath. Follow the footpath, soon widening into a track, still enclosed. Continue along the enclosed, unmetalled, track for half a mile as it descends into Monyash.

- Pass between farm buildings and our to the corner of a road. Keep ahead past '30 mph' signs for 75 yards, then turn right up Church Lane.

Monyash (its name means 'many ash' and refers to its wooded nature in the past) was once the centre of a flourishing agricultural community which also had an important lead mining industry associated with it. It was a prominent market town for the nearby farms in mediaeval times, and from 1340 onwards had a twice-yearly fair. In later days it became an important centre for the Quaker movement in Derbyshire.

- At the end of the lane, go through a squeeze stile into the churchyard

The parish church of St Leonard's was founded in the twelfth century, although most of it is fourteenth century in origin.

- Keep straight on through the churchyard to a squeeze stile by the gate opposite.

- Turn left down the lane to the village green.

The stump of the market cross can be seen on the green. It dates from 1340.

- At the cross roads beyond the green turn right back to the car park.

Stanton Moor: Bronze Age graves and fields

Distance: 4 miles

Map: OS sheet 119

Start and parking: The walk starts from the Red Lion Inn, in the middle of the village of Birchover (grid ref: 240622). Birchover is on a minor road, just off both the B5056 and the B5057, which roads in turn lead off the main A6 Matlock to Bakewell road. Birchover is approximately four miles south of Bakewell and four miles north of Matlock. There is effectively only one street to the village, and the Red Lion is in the middle of that street. There is ample parking on the roadside.

Refreshments: Public house and shops in Birchover.

Historical Background

For the four centuries from 1800BC to 1400BC, Stanton Moor was a place of sacred ritual for Bronze Age man. At the eastern end of the moor stands a circle of nine stones, the Nine Ladies, originally surrounded by an earthen bank. An entrance through the bank was marked by a single standing stone, pointing the way into the circle. Around the circle are over 70 burials sites, either mounds or circles walled with stones, each of which housed the remains of numerous cremated bodies.

But Stanton Moor was not only a burial ground for the dead. Equally importantly, it was a place for the living as well. The Moor is a broad shelf of land on the side of the Derwent valley, above the heavily forested valley floor and sheltered from the worst of the weather by the limestone plateau above it. Springs provided ample fresh water. Such shelves as these were the favoured sites for human habitation. They would have been covered with rich grassland and open woodland, not the peaty open moor of today. Earthen banks were built, partly as boundaries and partly to prevent soil erosion, and divided Stanton Moor into huge fields. Some of these were planted with a variety of crops, particularly cereals, and others set aside as pasture for grazing livestock.

Circular houses dotted the Moor, each one home to an extended family, with several generations living under the same roof. The stones cleared from the fields before cultivation were re-cycled to form burial mounds, or round barrows. These barrows contained representatives of the dead of one family only, not the dead of a whole community as earlier long barrows had done. The burial mounds were doted across the Moor, intermingling with the houses and fields of the community. Bronze Age man had a great feeling of oneness with nature. Like his stone age forebears, to him the dead were an on-going part of everyday life, and he saw no incongruity in growing his food amongst the graves of his ancestors. (see walk 2)

Over the centuries, continued planting of the same crops in the same fields, and continual deforestation, eventually depleted the soil. After 1400BC Stanton Moor was gradually abandoned as a place of settlement, and man moved to other locations.

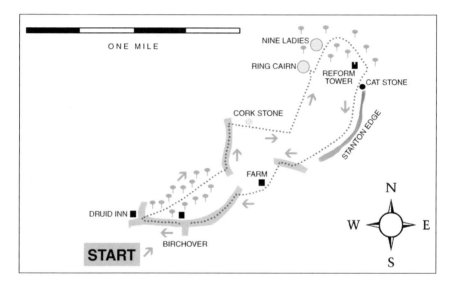

The Walk

This walk starts in the village of Birchover and crosses the small, open Stanton Moor, passing various Bronze Age sites, before returning past the nineteenth century Reform Tower.

● Standing with your back to the Red Lion, turn right down 'Main Street' (Birchover's main and almost only road.)

● Where the main road turns right, and opposite the ivy covered Druid Inn, turn right at a footpath post and climb a path into trees.

● Follow the path steeply uphill through trees, climbing the spine of a wooded ridge.

Nine Ladies Stone Circle.

- 600 yards from the Druid Inn, the footpath crosses open ground and reaches a road.
- Turn left along the road for 400 yards. Ignore a minor, unmarked track off to the right, but shortly after, turn right up a signposted footpath.
- In 30 yards cross a stile onto Stanton moor. Continue along a stony path, with a fence on the right.
- Pass the Corkstone, an isolated stone in front of a quarry on the left, now with metal hoops and footholes to facilitate climbing. Continue straight on along the path.
- 300 yards after the Corkstone, turn left at a crosstrack, signed to 'Nine Ladies stone circle'.

There are more than 70 Bronze Age burial mounds on Stanton Moor, recognisable to the untutored eye merely as low hummocks in the heather. The whole of this plateau was cleared for cultivation in the Bronze Age, and would have been covered with crops and the wooden huts of farmers, interspersed with the burial mounds.

- Continue ahead across the open moor, heading for open woodland ahead. After 500 yards, just before the edge of the wood is reached, deviate left for 50 yards along a clear path to an enclosure half hidden in the heather.

This enclosure is in fact a 'ring cairn', a stone embankment built to surround a low burial mound. Since most bodies were cremated and the ashes interred beneath mounds, very few remains of bodies have been found. Little is known about burial ceremonies in the Bronze Age, but one theory is that ring cairns were constructed to surround a funeral pyre, and the ashes subsequently interred within the circle. More formal burials were made within tumuli, burial mounds raised above a central, often stone lined, chamber. Only certain individuals were buried under mounds, and it is not known why some were chosen for such elaborate burial, whilst the rest were simply cremated in the open and their ashes scattered.

As well as human ashes, grave goods have also been found within these tumuli. These goods were not on the whole rich, no gold ornaments or the like having been found. Instead, they were pots containing food and drink, and a few simple tools. It is these pots that has given rise to the name by which these people are known, 'Beaker Folk. 'The goods appear to have been placed in the graves for the use of the dead in the afterlife, rather than to have commemorated their deeds in this life.

● Just inside the trees, bear slightly left of the path to the Nine Ladies stone circle.

The Nine Ladies Stone circle consists of 9 small stones set upright, within a 35 feet diameter stone bank, still just distinguishable. There were entrances through the embankment to the north-east and the south-west. Such embanked stone circles are not common in the British Isles, and are found mainly in Northern England.

A single insignificant standing stone, known as the Kings Stone, stands off to the south west. It is common to find an isolated 'pointer' stone associated with stone circles of this era.

The circle was a sacred site, where religious ceremonies would have taken place. By no means all of these ceremonies were to do with burying the dead, for many other 'rites of passage' were celebrated within the circle, rites connected with childbirth, puberty and marriage as well as death. The circle was there so that the community could celebrate the milestones of its individual members lives, in the presence of their ancestors. The stones acted as a mystical wall, to contain the magic of the occasion whilst excluding everyday life.

Bronze Age burials have often been found within such embanked circles, and a small mound in the middle of the Nine Ladies was excavated in the 18th century,but nothing was uncovered. Unlike the many ring cairns found on Stanton Moor, the purpose of the Nine Ladies Circle was not primarily for burial.It was a sacred site central to the whole vast burial complex, where religious ceremonies would have taken place.

There are more than seventy bronze age burial mounds on the 150 acre summit of Stanton Moor, together with ring cairns and the Nine Ladies. Ashes of 88 bodies have been found within 21 excavated mounds, together with a multitude of grave goods, including flint arrow heads and knives, bone beads, and bronze ornaments.

You may find it rewarding to wander around the summit in the vicinity of the Nine Ladies, and remember that the small mounds of earth, and occasional rings and mounds of stones, are the remains of a necropolis over 3500 years old.

● Just past the circle, turn right down a path to a stile.

● Cross the stile and turn right along a path, with a fence on your right and a steep drop with excellent views on your left.

● After a few hundred yards, pass the Reform Tower on your right.

This tower was erected in 1832 to commemorate the passing of the First Reform Act.

In 1830 the distribution of Parliamentary seats was wildly unrepresentative of the country, still reflecting the England of two hundred years previously. No account had been taken of the growth of the middle classes, nor of the development of new industrial towns. Nearby towns such as Sheffield, Derby, and Cromford were grossly under-represented.

In 1830 the right-wing Whig Earl Grey formed a new government pledged to parliamentary reform. The House of Commons eventually passed his Reform Bill, only for it to be defeated in the unelected House of Lords in October 1831. Riots broke out across England in protest: a mob broke into Derby gaol and released the prisoners; machines were smashed and mills burnt across the industrial north. There was a genuine fear of revolution, as had just been seen in neighbouring France. In the face of this King William IV reluctantly conceded to Grey's demands and created enough new peers to give the Prime Minister a majority in the Lords, and the Reform Bill was passed.

In reality the reforms enacted were modest enough, but the First Reform Act opened the door that would eventually allow the entry of parliamentary democracy as we know it today. The Reform Tower commemorates this historic event.

● Continue to follow the footpath along Stanton Edge, soon passing the Cat Stone, a large boulder with 'Ein 1831' engraved upon it, on your left.

● Follow the path as it curves right, away from the edge at the Cat Stone and leads back to a wire fence. Turn left along the fence, soon rejoining the edge.

● Continue with the fence on your right, following Stanton Edge for 600 yards as it curves to the right.

● Descend with the path to a lane.

● Turn right along the lane for 200 yards, then turn left through a squeeze stile at a footpath sign. Follow a path around the side of the hill and down towards a farm.

● Pass through a gate and descend, keeping to the left of farm buildings.

● Do not turn into the farmyard but instead pass to the left of the building in front, and then bear right to pass around the back of it.

● Keep a high wall on your right and pass through a field gate.

● Immediately past the gate turn right through a squeeze stile and continue ahead along a field, keeping the farm buildings away to the right.

● Join the track leading from the farm and keep straight on down the track, maintaining same line of advance. Follow the track to reach a road opposite the entrance to a stone finishing factory.

● Turn left down the road back into Birchover.

● 150 yards down the road, just past a church on the right, look out for a pinfold on your left.

Stray sheep and cattle were rounded up and kept in the village pinfold until their owner collected them and paid a fine for their release.

● Continue back down the main street to the Red Lion.

Mam Tor and the first arms race

Distance: 3.5 miles or 6 miles

Map: OS sheet 110

Start and parking: Car Park at Edale (grid ref: 124853). Edale is on a minor loop road off the A625, north of Hope, itself 12 miles west of Sheffield. The car park is on the junction of the loop road and the road leading into Edale village itself.

Refreshments: Public house and café 100 yards along the road into the village.

Historical Background

The Bronze Age in Europe saw the first ever arms race. At first the new bronze tools were no more resilient or effective than the stone tools already in use. Gradually however technology improved, and the metal implements became more and more effective at providing and retaining a sharp cutting edge. At the same time, an increasing population coincided with a decline in habitable land due to climatic changes. This resulted in increased competition for the space available. The new technology, initially used to provide household and agricultural tools, was soon utilised to provide weapons of war. These weapons themselves evolved: daggers lengthened into rapiers, which in turn were replaced by heavier-bladed swords more suitable for slashing at an enemy. Body armour, usually of stout leather, developed alongside these weapons, and for most of the Bronze Age this rendered the bow and arrow ineffective as a weapon. There were regional differences in the weaponry used, with the sword predominant in northern England, whilst over most of southern England, the spear became the favoured weapon. With the increased use of weapons a warrior elite came to dominate society, with a chief expert in the art of warfare at its head.

Inter-tribal warfare was as yet by no means endemic, and in many parts of Britain, especially the richer lowlands, neighbours peacefully co-existed. But in the upland areas, where agriculture was poorer and the pressure on land greater, the threat of violence grew. With it grew the need to provide a defensive site to which the population could withdraw in times of emergency. The earliest hillforts were built in the later Bronze Age, to provide a shelter in the event of attack.

The top of Mam Tor had been used as a burial site for the Bronze Age inhabitants of the Hope Valley for centuries. Sometime in the late Bronze Age it was fortified with a strong ditch and embankment, to provide a tribal sanctuary. The local population lived and worked in the arable land of the Hope and Noe valleys, with the hill-top usually providing a religious and administrative centre, but in times of emergency its ramparts were available for protection and defence, for both the people and their livestock.

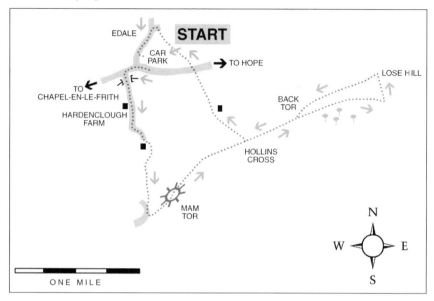

The Walk

This walk starts at Edale and climbs onto Mam Tor hill fort and along a splendid ridge to Hollins Cross. From here the walker can either return directly to Edale or add on a detour to Lose Hill, with its magnificent views to make a longer walk.

- Leave the car park onto the minor loop road you arrived along and turn right.

- Ignore a right turn into Edale village but keep ahead down the road in the direction of Chapel-en-le-Frith.

- In 80 yards turn left down a drive, at a National Trust sign for 'Hardenclough Farm'.

- Follow the drive across a bridge over the River Noe.

Mam Tor dominates the skyline in front. The line of embankment and ditch that protected the fort can be seen just below the summit of the Tor.

- Follow the drive for quarter of a mile, climbing steadily, to pass Hardenclough Farm on the right.

● Continue up the drive, now with a stream on your right. Ignore a stile and footpath on the right, but bear left with the drive to cross the stream.

● Climb with the drive. Just before the gates of a farm, turn left over a stile and immediately turn right onto a path signed 'Mam Tor'.

● Follow the enclosed bridleway as it winds uphill to a gate.

● Keep ahead after the gate. The path continues to wind uphill, soon crossing the bottom of open moorland, with a wall on the right.

● Follow the path, still with the wall on your right, up a gully, curving ever leftwards up the hillside.

It is worth pausing at intervals to look back. There are magnificent views over the valley of the Noe and up Edale to the Pennines behind. It also provides an excellent opportunity to get your breath back!

● At the top of the long gully cross a stile. Continue ahead up the path, soon cobbled and in a steep-sided gully, to reach a stile onto a road.

● Turn left up the road. Cross the summit and start to descend with the road. At the point where the road turns right, turn left at a National trust sign for 'Mam Tor'.

● Climb the stepped and fenced path to the top of Mam Tor. Follow the path to the triangulation point.

● From the trig point descend the path along the narrowing summit of the Tor.

The top of Mam Tor is 1695ft (517m) above sea level. Its name means 'Mother Mountain'. It was endowed with spiritual significance, for to Bronze Age man many natural locations were also places of religion and worship. Two Bronze Age burial mounds have been found on the summit, predating the building of the fort. In the late Bronze Age, possibly around 1000BC, the first defensive ditch and embankment was built, encircling the hilltop apart from to the east, where the vertical slope was protection enough. The land within the ramparts is unusual for a hillfort in that it is sloping rather than flat, and has over one hundred small platforms terraced into the slope, to provide level footings for circular huts built there. Pottery shards dating from between 1000-800BC were excavated here, as was a bronze axe.

Centuries later, in the Iron Age, the fortifications of Mam Tor were greatly strengthened. This was not a defensive necessity but was to emphasise the power of the local tribe. Hill forts were no longer simply places of defence in times of emergency, but were visible symbols of power and prestige, designed to overawe neighbouring tribes.

● After 300 yards pass through the ramparts of the fort in a gully.

It is worth clambering up to the top of the gully on the left of the path to gain the impression of the two encircling ramparts and intervening ditch, that surround the summit of the Tor on all but its sheer south-eastern face.

The original defensive earthworks consisted of a single rampart, surrounded by an outer ditch, with a further 'unofficial' bank developing over time beyond this, created by the periodic cleaning out and piling up of rubbish from the ditch. The initial Bronze Age fort would have had a timber palisade along the top of the bank. This was replaced in the Iron Age by a stronger rampart, with a vertical stone-faced outer side, which was later still strengthened even further at the entrance. The entrance was the weakest part of a hillfort. Here it is a sheer-sided alley 100 foot long, which would have been blocked by movable wooden structures, often just piles of logs.

There is no evidence that Mam Tor Hillfort ever saw action. During the Bronze Age and pre-Roman Iron Age the hillforts were symbols of power, and like the modern nuclear deterrent the all important thing was their existence not their use. The only force that could have reasonably hoped to take a fort such as Mam Tor was the Roman Legion, but the Brigantes of Derbyshire put up no real resistance to the advance of Rome in 80AD.

● Continue ahead along the ridge down a path, paved for erosion control.
The path you are now walking followed the old Bronze Age trail up into the hillfort. The most obvious route for cattle, goods and people to enter Mam Tor from the valleys below was up onto the saddle at Hollins Cross half a mile ahead, and then along the ridge you are on. In times of emergency the inhabitants of the valleys would have hurried along here three thousand years ago, carrying their meagre possessions and driving their valuable livestock before them, to the protective ramparts of the fort.

● At the end of the paved path, cross a stile and keep straight on down the ridge with a fence now on the left.

Mam Tor Hill Fort.

- Pass through a gate and keep straight on, now with a fence on the right and a tumbled-down wall on the left.

- At the end of the fence, pass between gateposts and keep straight on for 100 yards to the plinth in mid-path, at Hollins Cross.

A packhorse trail has crossed the ridge at this point since the middle ages, following the trail which man had used for 3000 years to travel between Edale and the Noe Valley to the north and the Hope Valley to the south.

For the shorter walk, turn off here.

- **For the longer walk,** keep straight ahead up the clear path, with a wall on the left and soon with a fence on the right.

- At the summit of the path cross a stile and keep straight on, now with a fence and soon a wall on your left, and the ridge dropping away on your right to Castleton.

- In 350 yards, just before woods on the right and crags on the left, DO NOT cross a stile on the left but continue straight on with the fence still on your left.

- In 100 yards cross a stile into the woods. Keep straight on through the trees on a clear path, to reach another stile.

- Cross the stile and keep straight on across open moorland, with the ridge up to your left. A stile soon becomes visible ahead.

- Cross the stile, signposted 'Hope' and keep ahead across the next field, curving slightly right to another stile.

- Cross this stile and follow the top of a field, with a wall on your left, to yet another stile.

- Cross this stile and keep straight on across the next field, maintaining height and avoiding turning downhill.

- Leave the field by a stile. Ignore a yellow waymark arrow, but instead turn left uphill, to a stile with a National Trust sign, 60 yards up the slope.

- Cross the stile by the National Trust sign and continue straight on up Lose Hill to the summit, on a path soon paved for erosion control.

From the summit of Lose Hill there are magnificent views in all directions, and a chance to gain a visual perspective of the history of this area. To the south-west looms the bulk of Mam Tor with its hill fort, the administrative centre of the area in the Bronze and Iron Ages. The valleys on either side would have been home to farmers and herdsmen, firstly of an unnamed Bronze Age people and, in the Iron Age, of the Brigantes. Down the valley to the south east, behind the concrete works at Hope, was the Roman fort of Navio. This was strategically placed to control both the main west-east route that ran down the Hope Valley, and the north-south route, which went southwards into Bradwell Dale visible behind Hope, and northwards behind the conical peak of Win Hill. To the south is Castleton, with Peveril Castle, the administrative centre of the Norman Peak Forest, clearly visible above it.

● From the summit turn left and walk along the ridge on a paved path. Follow the path to a stile.

● After the stile the path, no longer paved, is enclosed by a wall on the right and a fence on the left. Follow the path along the ridge to the summit of Back Tor.

From the summit of Back Tor, Mam Tor can be seen ahead, the double line of the defensive ramparts and intervening ditch clearly visible around the summit. The landslip scars on the left-hand face were present when the fort was built. The rampart was built up to the edge of them, thus incorporating the vertical slope into the defences of the fort. Subsequent slippage has slightly eroded the ramparts.

● Cross the summit of Back Tor and carefully pick your way down the crags. (This path is not dangerous, and nowhere near any drops, but the stones are loose and can be treacherous underfoot, especially in wet weather.)

● At the bottom of the crags, continue ahead with the fence on your left for 100 yards, to cross a stile on your left.

● Turn right along the track and, keeping the wall and later a fence on your right, retrace your steps for half a mile to Hollins Cross.

The route for both walks from Hollins Cross:

● From Hollins Cross turn northwards off the ridge (LEFT if coming from Mam Tor, RIGHT if coming from Lose Hill). DO NOT go through a gate on the right but follow the broad path downhill, with a wall on the right.

This is the old packhorse trail up from Edale.

● After 100 yards fork right downhill, signposted 'Edale'.

● Follow the path steeply downhill, to a stile to the left of a farmhouse.

● Cross the stile and keep straight on for 40 yards to reach a farm track.

● Turn left down the farm track. Follow the track as it descends, passing a barn on the left and winding downhill.

● Cross a stile by a field gate and follow the track across a bridge.

● 100 yards later, where the track curves to the right, keep straight on up the bank to a stile onto a road.

● Cross the road to a stile opposite, and keep straight on down the field, keeping the wall on your left.

● Halfway down the field, turn left through a squeeze stile at a footpath sign.

● Go half-right across the next field, to an arch under the railway.

● Go under the railway and keep straight on, with a wall on your left.

● In the corner of the field, turn left through a squeeze stile.

- Go half-right across the next field, aiming for a stile to the right of a barn ahead.
- Continue your line of advance across the next field, converging with a river bank and trees.
- In the top left corner of the field, turn left through a squeeze stile by a gate.
- Cross the river and keep straight on along a path, soon with a graveyard up the slope on the right. Follow the path out to a road.
- Turn left down the road for quarter of a mile, passing a public house and a café on your right. You soon come to the car park on your left.

Carl Wark: Hill forts in the Iron Age

Distance: 5 miles

Map: OS sheet 110

Start and parking: The walk starts from the free National Trust car park at Longshaw Country Park (grid ref: 267800). The park is on the B6065, 100 yards south of its junction with the A6187, four miles west of Sheffield.

Refreshments: The Fox House Inn is passed at the start of the walk. There is a tearoom at Longshaw County Park.

Historical Background

From 1000BC onwards the climate across the British Isles deteriorated, becoming colder and wetter. Destructive woodfelling had removed the protective tree cover, and the exposed soil became heavy and waterlogged, rapidly turning into an inhospitable peaty moor. By the same time the traditional areas of settlement, the sheltered arable shelves along the sides of the main river valleys, had become exhausted as after centuries of intensive farming the soil deteriorated. Many upland areas were abandoned and their inhabitants moved down into the fertile wooded valley bottoms. But by then the population had increased substantially, both on the uplands and in the lowlands, and competition for the available land increased dramatically (see walk 4).

This movement and increase in population coincided with the increased use of iron for tools and for weapons. Iron was easier to work than bronze, and iron ore was much more available. Consequently, iron weapons rapidly became readily available, and were used to settle the ever more frequent conflicts over land. For protection, families and tribes coalesced into loose confederations and petty kingdoms, headed by a ruling elite versed in the ways of war. Communities increasingly lived in the shadow of hill-forts, which could offer protection. These forts in turn were built ever larger and grander, a visible symbol of the power of the local ruler.

Derbyshire was home to the Brigantes, the largest of the British Iron Age tribes who occupied all of modern Yorkshire and Lancashire as well as Derbyshire. The Brigantes were a loose confederation of different tribes, nominally ruled over by one king but effectively with each tribe having a large degree of autonomy. Each tribe had its own power base in a locality, dominated by its own hill-fort. One such fort was Carl Wark, built in all probability at a later date than most other forts in the region. It displays advanced construction techniques and also shows evidence that it was built primarily for protection, not for prestige.

The Walk

This walk starts at Longshaw Estate, 1660 acres of country park well worth exploring, right on the Yorkshire border. It then crosses the county line for an

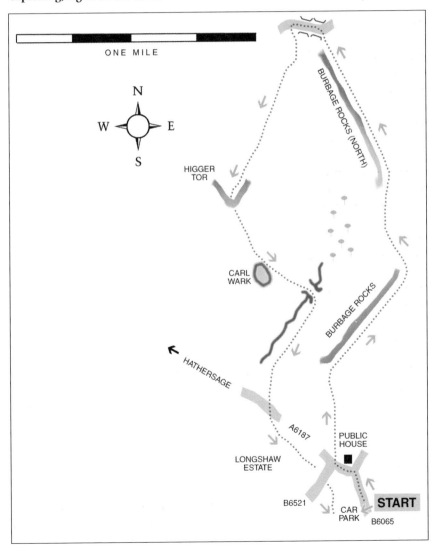

exhilarating walk along rocky valley edges and over moors to the iron age hillfort of Carl Wark, before returning again to Longshaw.

- ● Leave the car park and return to the B6065. Turn left along the road, back to the Fox House Inn, 100 yards away at the junction with the A6187.

- ● Turn left up the A6187 towards Hathersage. 50 yards past the end of the pub, turn right up a track through the bracken to a stile. (The turn is just behind a road sign on the right-hand side of the road.)

- ● Cross the stile and follow a clear track to cross a second stile in 40 yards.

- ● Follow a clear track through the heather over the moor, aiming for some prominent boulders seen ahead.

Carl Wark becomes visible in front of you on the other side of the valley, with Higger Tor behind it. In the Iron Age the scenery would have been much different. The warm temperate climate of the preceding millennia had changed. It had become much colder and wetter, and many of the previously farmed upland areas were being abandoned. The valley floor had previously been managed woodland interspersed with clearings for grazing and with the rectangular huts of the inhabitants. By the late Iron Age it was reverting to natural forest, thick and overgrown. The upland areas above had been farmed unremittingly for two thousand years and in consequence the soil was exhausted, and the natural tree cover destroyed. The peat bogs so all-prevailing today would not have fully formed, but the landscape was increasingly one of coarse grassland and embanked cultivated fields, more and more of which were being abandoned as the years progressed.

- ● Pass the boulders and continue ahead along the path for 100 yards, to meet a broad crossing track. Turn right along the track.

- ● At a cross track a few yards later, continue ahead along a broad track to the top of Burbage Rocks.

- ● There is a maze of minor paths through the heather and rocks on top of Burbage Rocks. It does not matter which one you follow, so long as you continue to walk along the edge of the rocks, with the edge on your left hand.

- ● Follow the top of Burbage Rocks for 1000 yards, soon with one path establishing itself as the major route along the edge.

- ● Where the first edge of rocks ends, take a clear cairned track that initially drops away left into the valley towards woods. The path soon has a ruined wall on its left.

- ● At a gully, swing right with the path to go along the edge of the northern part of Burbage Rocks, keeping the edge to your left, with trees in the valley below and Carl Wark and Higger Tor opposite.

- ● Follow the path as it divides and reunites, winding through boulders to reach the top of Burbage Rocks.

- Walk along the top of the Rocks, still with the edge on your left hand. The paths coagulate as one clear path through the heather, which you should follow out to a road.

- Turn left along the road for 200 yards, crossing two bridges in quick succession.

- Immediately after the second bridge, turn left to a stile at the back of an unsurfaced lay-by.

- Cross the stile. DO NOT go left down into the valley but take the right-hand path, staying to the edge above the top of the valley.

- Follow the clear path along the valley edge to Higger Tor. The path is stepped for erosion control near the top.

- At a cross track turn left, still with the edge on your left and the wooded valley below. Follow the path across the flat top of Higger Tor.

- Make for the large flat boulders at the end of Higger Tor and look down on Carl Wark.

From this vantage point the defensive construction of the Carl Wark hill fort can be readily appreciated. It stands on the end of a rocky outcrop, and can only be approached along the neck of the spur. A massive stone wall defended this approach.

The valleys below would have been home to an essentially farming community, living in permanent wooden houses, surrounded by their fields and by pastures for the cattle that were increasingly a symbol of a family's and a community's wealth.

It may seem odd that the fort would have been constructed on Carl Wark, overlooked as it is by the higher Higger Tor. However, in pre-artillery days, there was

The iron age fort of Carl Wark.

no way in which the occupants of Carl Wark could have been threatened by anyone on Higger Tor, which was well beyond the range of the bows and arrows in use in the Iron Age. Whether or not it was overlooked was thus irrelevant.

● Cross the boulders and pick your way carefully down to a broad track leading to Carl Wark.

● Climb into Carl Wark, passing a monumental dry-stone wall.

Carl Wark hill fort stands on a boulder-strewn crag, with steep and easily defended drops on all sides apart from this western one. A wooden palisade along the top of the crags would have been sufficient to defend the fort on the other three sides: here on the west a massive rampart of huge blocks of rock, nine feet high, was built on top of naturally occurring boulders, reinforced with an earthen embankment 20 feet wide to give a stable footing. The whole rampart is faced on the outside with dry-stone walling. There is no exterior ditch and rampart, such as is to be seen at Mam Tor (see walk 4). The interior area of the fort is small, less than two acres, and the rocky outcrops and boulders leave little room for settlement. Traces of hut circles and water troughs have been discovered, but on a scale that is too limited for more than occasional occupancy. This suggests that the fort was designed only to be used in an emergency, when immediate shelter was more important than comfort.

The construction of this fort is quite unlike anything else seen in Northern England, and there has been much speculation about its origin, the opinion even having been voiced that it dates from Neolithic times. This seems unlikely, and as the only remains of settlements found in the immediate vicinity are late Iron Age, it is most likely that the fort dates from this time, around 200BC. It would therefore have constructed by a people who were one of the tribes of the Brigantes confederation.

There is no evidence that Carl Wark was ever attacked. Although small, its excellent defences would have provided a massive deterrent to any attack by any of the surrounding tribes, and the Brigantes of Derbyshire, unlike their neighbours in Yorkshire and South Lancashire, put up little resistance to the Roman legions when they entered the region in 80AD.

It is worthwhile passing through the defensive wall and wandering around the fort, trying to picture the huts, cattle pounds and wooden ramparts that would have stood here over two thousand years ago.

● After inspecting the hillfort return to the dry stone wall and exit the fort, passing the wall on your left hand.

● Descend to a cross track in a few yards. Turn right and follow the track beneath the natural ramparts of Carl Wark.

Even today, the crags surrounding the Carl Wark plateau present a formidable barrier to entry. Two thousand years ago, with no vegetation on them and topped by a wooden palisade, they would have been impregnable.

● Follow the track down to an old packhorse bridge over a river, just to the right of woods.

- Cross the bridge, and keep ahead to cross a tributary stream by a plank bridge, and climb the bank opposite by steps.
- DO NOT turn half-left with the arrowed path. Instead turn right and follow a less distinct path along the side of the river valley.
- Follow the path to join a broader track at the base of rocks. Turn right along the track.
- Follow the track for quarter of a mile, through gates and out onto the road.
- Cross the road and go through a stile opposite, marked 'National Trust Longshaw'.
- Follow a clear track ahead through the woods, bearing left and with the road up to your left.
- Follow the path to a gate onto a road.
- Cross the road half-right to the vehicular entrance to Longshaw, with its gatehouse to the left.
- Go down the drive for 80 yards past the gatehouse, then turn left and take the right-hand most of two paths.
- Curve left with the path back to the car park.

The Longshaw estate is well worth exploring further. Longshaw Lodge was built in 1830 by the Duke of Rutland, who owned extensive land in Derbyshire including Haddon Hall (see walk 11). It was considerably extended later. It is surrounded by 1660 acres of woodland, moorland and farms, with varied walking and dramatic views. The Duke of Wellington and King George IV were regular visitors to the estate, riding, walking and hunting in its grounds. There is a Visitors Centre, with a café shop and information centre, and guided walks of the estate are available.

The Estate itself is open all year around. The Visitors Centre is open Easter to October, Wednesday-Sunday 11am-5pm: November to Easter, weekends only 11am-5pm.

Walk 6

Bradwell: the Romans invade

Distance: 3 miles

Map: OS sheet 110

Start and parking: The walk starts from the church of St Barnabas in Bradwell (grid ref: 173812). Bradwell is on the B6049, 3 miles south of Hope and 6 miles north of Tideswell. There is ample street parking in Bradwell.

Refreshments: Shops and public houses in Bradwell: The Travellers Rest public house is a hundred yards off route at the halfway mark.

Historical Background

The Romans landed at Richborough in Kent in 43AD. Their initial war aim was the destruction of the Catuvellaunian tribe, living in modern-day Essex, after which the legions swept north and west. By 54AD Rome occupied all the land south and east of a line from the Severn to the Humber as the new province of Britain. West of this were the hostile tribes of Wales. To the north, occupying all of modern Yorkshire, Lancashire and northern Derbyshire, were a confederation of tribes known collectively as the Brigantes.

Rome was initially happy for Brigantia to remain an independent client state, but in 69AD the Brigantes gained a new ruler, Venutius, openly hostile to the Romans and threatening the northern frontier of Roman Britain. Rome reacted to this threat by invading the territories of the Brigantes in 70AD. The initial thrust was up the east coast from the garrison town of Lincoln north to the Tyne. This was followed by a second thrust from Chester, up the west coast to the Solway. Since the tribesmen on the Peak were not amongst the most anti-Roman of the Brigantean clans, the area was ignored during the first invasion. However, the as the legions advanced further into Brigantia they needed to secure their rear, and in 78AD the Peak was occupied by the Romans with little resistance. The strategic importance of the Peak was reinforced when a major east-west road was built, crossing the Pennines through the Hope Valley. Spurs from this road criss-crossed the area to provide for rapid troop deployment.

As well as the strategic consideration, Derbyshire was attractive to the Romans as a source of lead, an extremely important commodity. The Peak became one of the most important sources of lead for the Romans. Ingots produced in the area and bearing the word 'Lutudarum' were to be found all over the Empire, Lutadarum being thought to be the name of the administrative centre of the lead-mining industry.

To defend its lead mines, and to hold down the newly conquered lands, the Romans built several forts. One such was at Navio, near present-day Hope.

The Walk

This short walk passes the medieval embankment known as the Grey Ditch and visiting the remains of Navio Roman fort before returning across the hillside, with fine views to Bradwell.

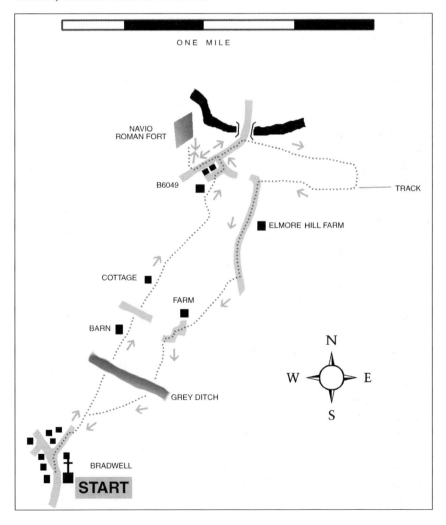

● Standing in the main street of Bradwell, facing the church of St Barnabas, turn left down the main road.

● In 50 yards turn right down Soft Water Lane.

Derbyshire has truly been called 'the cradle of the Industrial Revolution'. Even before Richard Arkwright introduced his revolutionary new machinery and factory methods at Cromford (see walk 20), there had been a multitude of small mills, owned and worked by single families, utilising the power of the fast-flowing streams of the peaks to drive their millwheels and spin their cotton yarn. Along this short lane two such mills utilised the waters of Bradwell Dale to soften the raw cotton before converting it to yarn.

● Keep ahead, with the mill stream on your left, passing two mills on your left.

● Pass Butts Mill Court on your left and 10 yards later take a footpath on the right.

● Keep along the bottom of the next small field and leave through a squeeze stile.

● Cross the next field, aiming just to the right of a concrete shed seen ahead, to go through a pedestrian gate.

● Continue straight on, passing the shed on your left. With a wall on your left go along the bottom of the next field.

● Go through a pedestrian gate and cross the next small field to a squeeze stile.

● Go through the squeeze stile and maintain your line of advance to pass through a band of trees and across the next field to a kissing gate.

● Maintain the same line of advance across the next field. In 50 yards you pass through a large embankment running down the field across your path.

This embankment is the Grey Ditch, which originally extended across the full width of the Bradwell Valley.

Angles and Saxons from Germany and the low countries started to enter England in increasing numbers between 400-600AD. They arrived in waves through Kent and East Anglia, pushing ever westwards and displacing the native Britons before them. AD England south and east of the line from the Bristol Channel to the Humber, and up the eastern side of the Pennines, was Anglo-Saxon. The original British still survived as a separate entity west of the Pennines, and a smell enclave, known as the Pecsaete or 'People of the Peak' remained on the limestone uplands of the White Peak, south of the Hope Valley.

Both the origins and purpose of the Grey Ditch are now lost in the mists of time, but it is likely it was constructed sometime in the seventh century, and marked the boundary between the lands of the Pecsaete to the south and the Anglo-Saxons to the north-east, who had penetrated the Peak District along the Hope Valley. Although it would have originally have been higher and steeper than it is today, it is most unlikely that the embankment was ever intended to be defended. It is much more

The dark age embankment, the Grey Ditch.

likely to have been built as a marker, in much the same way that Offa's Dyke was built along Mercia's western border.

- Continue the same line of advance to a squeeze stile with stepping stones.
- Cross the next field, aiming for a gap in the hedge, just to the right of some corrugated iron barns.
- Go along the bottom of the next field to a gated squeeze stile.
- Keep straight on across the next field, passing just to the right of a line of trees in mid-field. At the end of the trees cross a stile into a lane.
- Cross the lane to a squeeze stile opposite and continue straight on along the bottom of the field, with a hedge and fence on your left.
- Leave the field by a pedestrian gate just beyond a cottage on the left. Keep straight on across the next field, aiming for a stile just to the left of a prominent tree 50 yards ahead.
- Cross the stile and keep straight on across the next field, to a stile by a gate halfway along the bottom, left-hand boundary.
- Cross the stile and maintain your previous line of advance, now with the hedge on your right.
- Follow the hedge then a fence, to cross a stile by a gate at the end of the field.
- Continue along the track for 80 yards then cross a stile ahead, by a gate.
- Keep straight on, keeping the hedge to your left. Where the hedge turns left in mid-field, turn left and follow, still with the hedge on your left.

- At the bottom of the field turn right and follow the field boundary, still with the hedge on your right, now with buildings behind it.
- Follow the field track to a pedestrian gate beside a field gate.
- Go through gate and keep ahead for 25 yards, then turn right in front of buildings. Follow the drive out to a lane.
- Turn left for 10 yards to reach a more major road.
- Cross this road and turn left. In 15 yards cross a stream.
- Immediately after the stream, turn right through a gate, and cross a small paddock to a stile.
- Keep straight on across the next field to a ladder stile by a gate.
- Cross the ladder stile to view all that remains of the roman fort of Navio.

Navio was built soon after the Brigantes had been crushed in 70AD. It was built in the heart of the territory of a Brigantean tribe whose lands were based upon nearby Mam Tor hillfort (see walk 4), and it remained in use for several centuries. It was strategically positioned at a junction of newly constructed Roman roads, where the east-west route along the Hope Valley, connecting the fort at Melandra (Glossop) with Chesterfield, joined the southern route through the Batham gate and up the Bradwell Valley to Buxton. Eventually a northern spur was constructed off the east-west road, to join the main east coast highways near present-day Rotherham.

After the might of the Roman Legions had been used to crush any resistance, it fell to auxiliary troops to garrison and police the newly occupied lands. Auxiliaries were recruited from amongst newly conquered peoples, who were then posted to distant parts of the Empire for duty, where they would not have sympathy with the local population and would be less inclined to jeopardise their chances of returning home by rebellion. It is known that for a part of its history Navio was garrisoned by Gauls, recruited in Aquitaine in south-west France. Auxiliaries were more lightly armoured than the heavy shock-troops of the regular legions, and often retained their own regional speciality in weaponry. In the case of the Gauls at Navio this was a light javelin, a large two-edged sword and a small round leather shield.

The fort at Navio was typical of those built to house auxiliaries. It was along the same lines as a legionary base, but much smaller in size, being only three acres in area. It was broadly square in shape, surrounded by two rings of stout walls with ditches outside, the innermost wall being some twenty feet high and topped with a wooden palisade. Initially the walls were of earth and wood, which were eventually replaced with stone. There was a gate in each wall, and inside the fort were barracks, storehouses, cookhouses and a headquarters block. The other amenities required by the troops, including bath-houses and temples, were built outside the walls. Navio would have housed an auxiliary infantry cohort of 500 men.

In time a 'vicus' or civilian town grew up outside its walls, where the local population were encouraged to settle and engage in trade and manufacturing. Not only did the vicus service the garrison, but the introduction of the benefits of urbanisation to conquered tribal people was also a deliberate policy by the Romans. Good housing, education, cultural amenities, and markets were all designed to lock the local population into a Roman way of life.

Today only the embankments of the fort walls, around the flat central area, are left. It requires an exercise of the imagination to picture the Roman fort that stood here.

● After viewing Navio, return to the road and turn left.

● Keep ahead down the road for 200 yards, passing an agricultural merchants on the left.

Note the millstones set into the gateposts. Millstone manufacture was a major industry in the Peak District.

● Immediately before the bridge, cross the road. Cross the wall on the right hand side of the road, just this side of the bridge, using stone steps set into the wall itself.

This design of ladder stile, utilising the actual bricks with which the wall is built to provide the steps, is a hallmark of the original walls in the Peak District.

● Follow an overgrown path along the river bank to a pedestrian gate.

● Go quarter-right across the field, to a squeeze stile by a field gate.

● Go over the stile and then half-right up the bank. Eventually a stile comes into view on the skyline.

● To reach this stile, ignore an inviting gate ahead but follow the field boundary, passing the gate on your left and continue up the slope, with a stand of young trees on the left-hand side. Climb steeply up the bank to the stile by an indicator post.

● Cross the stile and go straight ahead across the field. A radio mast on the hill ahead indicates the direction to go in.

● On the far side of the field, turn right along a track.

● Pass a green metal field gate on the left and then go through a wooden gate ahead.

There is an excellent view over Hope and up the Hope Valley to the Lose Hill ridge.

● Go down the steep track and through a squeeze stile by a gate. 20 yards later, cross another stile by a second gate.

● Keep straight on along the track for 100 yards, to a corner of a metalled lane. Turn left uphill.

● Where the metalled drive turns left into Elmore Hill Farm, keep ahead up the unmade track for 100 yards, to a squeeze stile in the right-hand hedge.

● Go through the stile and half-left around the slope. The path soon becomes more distinct and shortly, when Bradwell becomes visible ahead, starts to drop.

- Cross a ladder stile by a gate and descend to a pedestrian gate beside a field gate, with a farm and corrugated iron barn to the right.
- Go through the gate and up the bank. Keep ahead along the bottom of the field, with a hedge on your right, to reach a stile.
- Cross the stile and turn left along a farm track.
- Follow the track as it bends sharp right and then left, and then descends. Where the track bends sharp right again, cross a stile in the left-hand fence.
- Go along the bottom of the field, with a hedge on your right.
- Cross a stile in the far right hand corner of the field.

The embankment of the Grey Ditch is in the field in front of you.

- Go half-right down the slope, aiming for a kissing gate in the hedge ahead, midway between telegraph poles.
- Maintain your line of advance across the next field and pass through a band of trees.
- Maintain the same line of advance to a stile ahead.
- Turn left through the stile and then retrace your outward steps along the right hand edge of four small fields, to emerge onto Soft Water Lane again.
- Turn left along the lane back to the main road.
- Turn left back to the church.

Roystone Grange: farming through the centuries

Distance: 3.5 miles

Map: OS sheet 119

Start and parking: The walk starts from a free car park (grid ref: 194582), on a minor road just south of the hamlet of Pikehall, on the A5012. Pikehall is 8 miles west of Cromford on the Buxton road. The car park is threequarters of a mile south of Pikehall along a minor road to Parwich.

Refreshments: None

Historical Background

The area of modern-day Derbyshire was brought under Roman control rapidly and peacefully. The lowlands of the Trent valley were controlled within ten years of the Romans landing in Kent in 43AD, and the uplands of the Peak occupied by 80AD at the latest. Whether the occupation was initially welcomed or ignored by the existing British population is unknown, but part of the roman genius was in getting an occupied race to accept the benefits of roman civilisation and thus fight to preserve it. The romans had no prejudice against race or colour, and easily assimilated local populations into the Empire.

There is no evidence in Derbyshire of a roman elite based upon affluent villas such as existed further south. Instead society was based upon farms or hamlets, which retained much of the character of iron age. Settlements consisted of several rectangular buildings, with yards, gardens lanes and fields around them. The farms were owned by local Britons, who prospered under the roman occupation. They benefited from good communications and a buoyant economy created by increased markets abroad and the need to service local garrison. This prosperity was reflected in the richer and better designed houses, the rich jewellery and other goods, and a more civilised lifestyle.

Although the prosperity of the area diminished with the declining fortunes of the Roman Empire, this romanised British society continued to flourish in Derbyshire long after the romans departed in 410AD. Over the next two centuries increasing immigration by Anglo-Saxons led to the lowlands being fully anglicised by 600AD. However, the original British inhabitants of the area continued to retain their separate identity on the White Peak until well into the eighth century.

Subsequent building and farming have buried all traces of Romano-British society remains on the Derbyshire lowlands, but the remains of about 50 farms still survive across the Peak, mainly on the limestone plateau. Of these the best example is at Roystone Grange, where the fascinating development of a community from roman times to the present day can be traced.

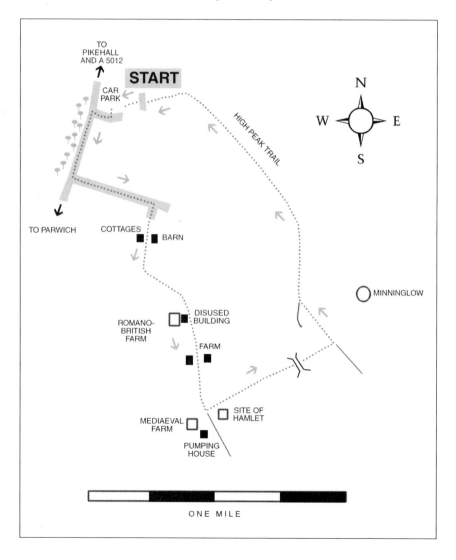

The Walk

This short walk goes through open fields, passing sites that have been farmed for the past 5,000 years, before returning along the High Peak Trail.

● From the car park entrance turn right in the lane. 50 yards later, at a T-junction, turn left in the direction of Parwich.

● After 400 yards, where trees on the right end at a track, turn left up a minor road.

The conspicuous mound seen on the horizon ahead, topped with a clump of trees, is Minninglow, a Neolithic burial mound built originally about 3500BC and repeatedly added to over the next thousand years. The tomb originally consisted of one large chamber, stone lined and covered with an earthen mound. This was later extended, by driving a corridor to the rear with four extra chambers leading off it, and the covering mound being elongated. Later still this was extended again, to create a massive nearly circular mound.

By 3500BC Neolithic man had ceased to be a nomadic hunter-gatherer, and had settled down to practice farming in a specific area. They were few in number, and probably lived in social groups based around an extended family, a family that included the dead as well as the living. It seems likely that prehistoric man practiced some form of ancestor worship or at least reveration. The dead were present, in soul, spirit, call it what you will, and provided an on-going link between the present and the past (see walks 2 and 3).

The conspicuous airy site for this tomb was chosen not only for religious reasons but also for territorial ones: the visual presence of the tomb announced the long-term inter-connection between a people and a specific area of land. Although the burial chambers at Minninglow have long since disappeared, looted by past hunters of mythical treasure, the huge mound still dominates the landscape, an on-going reminder of those first farmers who worked this land 5,000 years ago.

● After 600 yards, turn right through a gate and go down a drive towards a farm seen ahead.

● Pass between cottages on the right and a barn on the left, and go through a gate ahead.

● Continue along the track, winding through a pleasant valley.

● Cross a cattle grid. Go forward for 200 yards to a disused farm building on the right.

● Go just past the building, then climb up from the track to the building. Behind the building, look over the wall to see the remains of a Romano-British farm (an information plaque on the building will show you that you are in the right place.)

The original farmhouse that stood here was built in the second century AD, by a

Briton from the Midlands who been attracted north by the prospect of cheap land. It was constructed with rubble-filled walls, rectangular in basic outline but with bow-shaped walls. It was 20 yards long and 12 yards wide at its broadest part, with one main hall and side rooms for sleeping. It had a thatched roof, supported by a line of posts in two aisles down either side of the building. Behind the farmhouse was its own farmyard and garden plot, surrounded by walls built of 'orthostats', large stones and boulders carefully positioned to form a dry-stone wall. (an example of this will be seen later in the walk). Around the farmhouse was a small hamlet for the owners' workers, mainly freemen. Two large fields were laid out around the farm and extending down the valley, where sheep were bred for wool. At the southern end of the valley the fields were terraced, and worked for cereals by farm labourers. Lead was also mined, open-cast, on a small scale on these lands. At least 50 adults lived and worked in this valley compared to ten today.

This was a rich farm: polished tableware, and jewellery from the farther reaches of the Empire have been found here. The builder of the farm, although a Briton by birth, had fully espoused roman values and the roman way of life, and had been enticed northwards as part of the roman policy of extending their civilisation into the wilder borders of their province. But although rich for the area, the farm never equalled the affluence of its southern counterparts, and never acquired the mosaic floors or central heating commonly associated with roman villas.

The fortunes of the farmstead declined over time, and by the end of the third or the beginning of the fourth century AD the building had been levelled and a more modest farmhouse built in its place. Far smaller flocks of sheep now grazed the immediate hillside, and down the valley the fields had been subdivided by low banks into allotments for another four individual families, each with their own small house, who existed largely by subsistence farming.

The low retaining wall and post holes of the original second-century farm building can still be seen if you look over the wall behind the disused dairy.

- Return to the track and continue along it, shortly passing a barn down on the left and soon going through a modern farm complex.
- Continue along the track. Pass a footpath post and step stile on the left and continue forward to the church-like building ahead.

This building was in fact a pumping house, built in the nineteenth century to send air to pneumatic drills used in the quarries further down the track.

On the hillside behind the pumping house is a spring of fresh water. It was the presence of this spring, the only one in the valley, that induced a local landowner, Adam of Herthill to build a farm, called Revenstones, here, in the early twelfth century.

Henry II (reigned 1154-1189) granted land in the Royal park of the Peak to the rich monastic orders of the south, to entice them to establish communities in Derbyshire and to develop sheep farming and wool production, to support the *growing English textile trade. One such monastic order, The Cistercian monks from Garendon Abbey in Leicestershire, acquired the lands of Revenstone and proceeded to develop a new community, Roystone grange (the word 'grange' means a farm of monastic origin).*

Thirty yards behind the pumphouse are low grass-covered walls, all that remain of the mediaeval grange. It was built in a L shape, the originally body being an aisled timber roofed Hall, with a barn adjoining. The hall was later converted into a two roomed stone hall, and the barn into a dairy. Sheep pens were built adjoining the grange. The monastic lands covered 400 acres, and as well as a core of monks the grange had a number of lay-brothers, mainly local people, to work as shepherds and farm labourers. The grange supported more than 50 people in its heyday, but by 1400AD a long series of cold wet winters had rendered the grange unprofitable, and it was abandoned.

After the Dissolution of the Monasteries in 1536 the lands of the Catholic Church were seized by the crown. Roystone Grange was given to a local farmer, Rowland Babington. It is ironic that a distant relative of his, Anthony Babington, would 50 years later die trying to restore a Catholic monarch to the throne of England (see walk 14).

- ● After looking at the grange, retrace your steps for 20 yards, and cross the step stile in the wall passed earlier, now on your right, beside a footpath post.
- ● Cross the field to a squeeze stile in the wall opposite.

The humps and bumps in this field are the remains of the walls of a hamlet which grew up in the sixteenth, seventeenth and eighteenth centuries. This was a small farming community, existing by the subsistence farming of a few pigs, cereals and vegetables. They would also have looked after the sheep which still grazed the valley, owning a few themselves but mainly looking after the flocks of their landlord, Rowland Babington's descendants.

The hamlet was eventually pulled down in the late eighteenth century, and the stones reused to build the modern farmhouse.

- ● Go through the stile and turn left. Go up the side of the field, keeping the wall on your left, and pass through a gate.
- ● Continue up a track, with the wall still on the left hand side.
- ● Just before the next gateway, cross the wall on the left over a step stile beside a footpath sign.

Immediately over the stile, turn to look at the construction of the wall you have crossed. You will see modern dry-stone walling, using comparatively small stones, on top of much larger, boulder like stones. These are 'orthostats', part of the original second-century roman walls that formed a great circle around the hill to the south and marked the boundary of one of the two great fields of that day. The stones that formed the base of that wall have been in position for the last 1,800 years, a credit to the skill of those ancient wall-builders.

Roystone Grange, farmed for 2000 years.

- Once over the stile, continue your previous line of advance up the field, now with the wall on your right hand.

- Pass through a squeeze stile beside a gate and continue ahead to an archway beneath the High Peak Trail.

- After passing through the arch, continue the same line of advance up the field, keeping the faint outline of a ruined, grass-covered wall on your left hand.

This wall was the boundary of the mediaeval Roystone Grange. A trackway has followed this boundary wall along where you are now walking since at least 1160AD.

- Make for a footpath signpost visible in the wall ahead, some 30 yards to the right of the ruined wall. Cross a step stile at this signpost.

- Turn left down an enclosed trackway.

This was the route of the Cromford and High Peak Railway (see walk 20), built in 1831 to connect the Peak Forest Canal with the Cromford Canal. It ran for 33 miles through the quiet farmland of the High Peak, and the effect it had upon this tranquil valley, which had seen little but farming for five thousand years, must have been devastating.

- Follow the trackway to a gate. Pass through the gate onto the High Peak Trail. Turn right and pass through another gate in 10 yards.

- Follow the enclosed High Peak Trail for a mile, in the process crossing an airy viaduct.

En route you pass a disused quarry, where once limestone was extracted. Initially the High Peak Railway was used to transport limestone from the interior of the White

Peak to the canal and hence to the rest of England. As demand for limestone increased, quarries were developed on the side of the railway, making for cheap and efficient transportation of the stone.

On route note the viaducts, built to carry the railway on a level across the valley bottoms. Whatever the effect of the railway, these are magnificent feats of Victorian civil engineering.

● After a mile cross a minor road and enter the car park.

Walk 8

Bakewell and the unification of England 920 AD

Distance: 3.5 miles

Map: OS sheet 119

Start and parking: There are a number of car parks in Bakewell, all pay & display. It is recommended that you park in the long stay car park, which is at the far end of the town bridge, where the A619 and the B6408 meet before entering Bakewell. Do not be confused that the car park is signed as both 'car park' and 'industrial estate'. The walk starts from the edge of the car park, (grid ref: 220686).

Refreshments: Shops, tearooms and public houses in Bakewell.

Historical Background

In the seventh century the Peak District was the northern periphery of Anglo-Saxon power. From the lowlands of the Trent valley southwards were the Christian powers of the Anglo-Saxons, whilst to the north and east was the kingdom of York, ruled by pagan norsemen. In between were a people, over 1,200 families, known as Pecsaetans, or 'Peak Dwellers', survivors of the original British inhabitants of England who had lived here ever since Roman times. Gradually Anglo-Saxons from Mercia moved onto the Peak, initially as a ruling elite but eventually as migrants. A warlord of these newcomers, Badeca, made his home near a spring or well in the valley of the Wye, at a point where the Wye was fordable, which soon became known as Badeca's Well or Bakewell. Gradually the Anglo-Saxon kingdom of Mercia extended its frontiers northwards, incorporating the Peak District and using it as a buffer zone between Mercia and its neighbours.

In 914AD Edward the Elder, who had succeeded his father Alfred the Great as king of Wessex, embarked upon a campaign to unite the many Anglo-Saxon kingdoms into one. He and his sister Elfreda, a redoubtable general in her own right, campaigned northwards and eastwards in two great sweeps lasting for six years. They gained land by conquest or diplomacy from the other Anglo-Saxon kingdoms or from the norsemen and held it by building a series of fortresses. The

Danish stronghold of Derby was captured in 917AD, and in 920AD Edward reached Bakewell. Here he erected a strong fortress on the site of an old iron age fort. He called to Bakewell representatives from all the surrounding kingdoms, the Scots, the Norsemen of Northumbria and Strathcyde and the Anglo-Saxon kingdoms. After much debate this 'summit meeting' settled many outstanding border disputes and cleared the way for a more peaceful co-existence. Edward was elected 'father and lord', or overlord of those present, the first real ruler of all England, although it fell to his son and heir, Athelstan, to be the first man to be acknowledged as King of England.

The Walk

This walk goes around the historic sites of the old town of Bakewell before climbing onto the moors above the town and returning along the Monsal Trail.

● Leave the long stay car park and make your way to the old town bridge, which carries the main road (A619) into Bakewell.

Although the original town bridge was widened in the nineteenth century, its mediaeval structure can still be seen. It was built to be wide enough for a laden horse-drawn cart to cross, with alcoves for pedestrians to shelter in to avoid being crushed.

● Cross over the busy bridge with care, staying on the narrow left hand pavement. Continue straight on along Bridge Street, passing the Old Market Hall (now housing the Tourist Information Office) on the left and the Wheatsheaf pub on the right.

The Old Market Hall has the gables and two-mullioned windows typical of its seventieth century origin. On its façade are the coats of arms of several prominent local families, including the Vernons and the Manners, owners of Haddon Hall and effectively rulers of this area (see walk 11). Originally it would have been open-arched, allowing the business of the adjoining market to have been carried out within its shelter. The arches were bricked up in the eighteenth century. From 1827 until 1881 it was used as the Town Hall of Bakewell.

● Continue straight on across traffic lights into Rutland Square, with the war memorial in the centre and the Rutland Arms Hotel facing you.

The Rutland Arms was built in 1805 on the site of a former coaching inn of the same name. It was built as part of a speculative venture by the Duke of Rutland, who had plans to develop Bakewell as a spa town to rival the success of nearby Buxton (see walk 23). Jane Austen stayed in this inn several times – the bedroom she used still exists – and she used the inn in Pride and Prejudice *as one of the meeting places between Elizabeth Bennett and Mr Bingley. The town of Lambton in the novel is based upon Bakewell. It was in the Rutland Arms that Bakewell Pudding (commonly miscalled 'tart') was invented in 1860, when a harassed cook put together the ingredients for a strawberry tart in the wrong order. The dish was an instant success.*

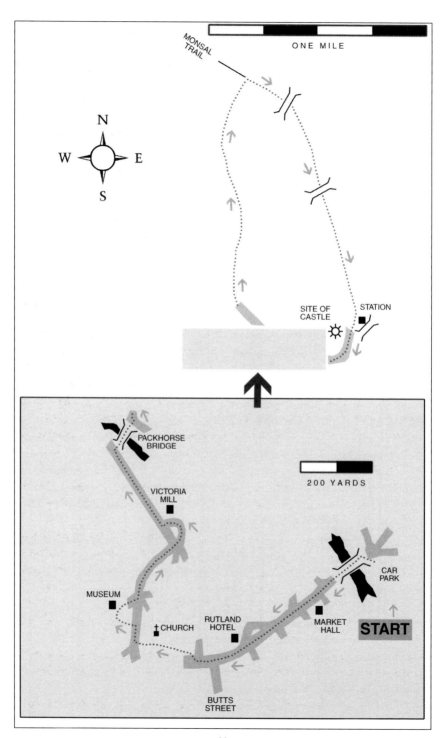

ONE MILE

MONSAL TRAIL

N
W — E
S

SITE OF CASTLE

STATION

PACKHORSE BRIDGE

200 YARDS

VICTORIA MILL

MUSEUM

† CHURCH

RUTLAND HOTEL

MARKET HALL

CAR PARK

START

BUTTS STREET

● Cross over the A6/Matlock Road at pedestrian lights and go down King Street, at the side of the Rutland Arms.

● 50 yards down Kings Street is the Old Town Hall facing you on the right, and on the left opposite it is the Cadcliffe House, now housing the Job Centre.

Cadcliffe House is a fine example of the town houses built in the mid eighteenth century by industrialists and merchants of Bakewell, and buildings of this sort, which abound in the town, reflect the wealth generated by the industrial revolution.

● Cross Butts Street and continue straight on up South Church Street, passing the St Johns Hospital almshouses on the right opposite Butts Street.

The name of Butts Street indicates the roads mediaeval past. During the Hundred Years War, England developed the longbow, a weapon which was to dominate the battlefields of Europe for 200 years. In skilled hands this weapon could drive a metal tipped arrow through the thickest armour at a range of 250 yards, and thus ended the dominance of the mounted knight. To ensure this skill every commoner was required, on pain of fines, to practice with the longbow for two hours every week, after the Sunday church service was finished. An area was set aside for this practice, usually waste ground abutting the town walls and near to the church. The straw targets used were known as 'butts', and the practice areas were called after them.

The original St Johns Hospital was built on this site in 1602. Not a 'hospital' in todays sense of the word, but rather a 'hospice', the building was to provide accommodation in a barrack-like building for six 'worthy poor' old men of the borough. They lived in spartan conditions under an almost military regime and were required to wear a uniform – a gown with the blue and yellow cross of St John on the breast- in return for the charity they received. The original hospital was pulled down in 1709 and six almshouses erected in its place, which provided private dwellings for the poor. The building is still used as an almshouse, although now it has been modernised into three homes.

● Fifty yards beyond Butts Street, on the opposite side of the street and at the end of the alms houses, turn right up Church Alley and enter the churchyard via steps and an iron gate.

All Saints Church was built in the Norman era, on a site used for Christian worship since Saxon times, and the original Norman west door still remains. It was extended in the thirteenth century, and a spire added to the Norman tower in the fourteenth century. The church was extensively renovated in 1841-52, when the original spire and tower was pulled down and replaced by the present one. The church contains a memorial chapel to the Vernon and Manners families, the 'Kings of the Peak' who lived in nearby Haddon Hall (see walk 11).

● Climb up the churchyard towards the church and turn left along a path, to pass the church on your right. Against the church wall, enclosed in iron railings, is the Saxon Cross.

After the Romans withdrew from Britain, the Christian religion they had introduced was driven underground as waves of pagan invaders swept in from Scandinavia, Germany and the Low Countries. When Christian missionaries started to re-establish Christian worship in northern England from the seventh century onwards, they found no formal churches left, and so had to preach on the open moors. Preaching crosses were erected at strategic points on the moors to mark where congregations should gather to listen to itinerant preachers.

The mutilated remains of the Saxon cross here at Bakewell are still magnificent, with panels illustrating the Annunciation and the Crucifixion. The cross would have originally been much larger, probably 12 to 14 feet high, and would have been painted to highlight the religious images. It did not originally stand here, but was moved into the churchyard to preserve it. More than 30 such crosses have been found in the Peak District, the richest collection of Anglo-Saxon sculpture in England outside Durham. Another magnificent cross can be seen at Eyam (walk 16).

● Continue up the side of the church, pausing to view another cross just to the right of the path, in front of the south porch.

This second cross originally stood on Harewood Moor, east of Beeley.

It is worth detouring down to the south porch to view the stone coffins leant against the outside wall.

● Return to the path and continue your former direction, to exit the churchyard via a stone arch, to emerge opposite a sign saying 'Parsonage Croft'.

● Turn right, with the churchyard on your right hand. After 50 yards turn left up an alley signposted 'museum'.

The town museum is in a fifteenth century yeoman's house, the affluent dwelling of a rich yeoman farmer of the area. In 1777 it was leased to Richard Arkwright (see walk 20), who built a mill in Bakewell. He converted the property into ten dwellings for mill employees. Today it houses a museum of Bakewell life through the ages.

● Turn right and pass along the front of the museum and continue down a lane.

● Where the lane emerges at a cross roads with the junction of North Church Street, turn left, and 30 yards later turn right down Fly Hill.

● Pass the YHA on your right and continue straight on down a very steep alley, with an iron handrail down its right-hand wall.

● At the bottom of the alley turn left and follow Bagshaw Hill out to the main road.

● Cross over the main road and curve left around a quiet crescent, passing the Milford House Hotel on your right. At the entrance to Milford Garage, pause to look at the mill race on your right. Behind the wall to the left, underneath which the mill race runs, is Victoria Mill.

● Follow the crescent out to the main road and turn right.

● Look over the wall on your right into the yard of Victoria Mill. There is the old iron millwheel standing in the yard.

Saxon Cross in Bakewell Churchyard.

Victoria Mill stands on the site of an old Saxon cornmill: there had been a cornmill here since the time of the Doomsday Book, utilising the power of an artificially created mill race to grind corn. With the coming of the Industrial Revolution, and the harnessing of water power to drive heavy machinery in the new factories, the corn mill was converted into a textile factory. The mill race was deepened and the gradient increased for greater water speed and therefore power to drive the new iron millwheel.

- Continue up the right-hand side of the main road, with the mill race, now much overgrown, on your right. After 200 yards, turn right to cross the mill race.

Note the Sheep Pound over the wall on your left. Stray sheep and cattle were rounded up and compounded in the sheep pound until such time as their owner paid a fine for their release.

- Follow the path across the packhorse bridge over the River Wye to reach a road.

The packhorse bridge was built here in 1664. Before the building of turnpike roads, transport in the valleys and peaks of Derbyshire was slow and prone to interruption by adverse weather. Horses were the only way to transport heavy goods. Often long trains of up to 100 horses haltered together were led by a muleteer and his assistants. Loads of up to two-hundredweight were carried in wicker panniers, slung on either side of the horse. Bridges were built to cross the many fast and deep streams of the area, which were constructed to be just wide enough for a laden packhorse to cross.

- Cross the road and continue straight up the lane opposite.
- Follow the lane as it climbs uphill, passing an ex-railway arch on your right. At the end of the lane continue ahead up a track into trees.
- Follow the track through a metal gate and up a field. Where the track turns left into a disused quarry, keep straight on, crossing grass to a squeeze stile beside a metal field gate.
- Go through the stile and continue ahead up an enclosed green lane.

There are fine views back over Bakewell at this point.

- Cross a ladder stile beside a gate and continue up the green lane. Follow the lane into a field and keep straight on, with a wall on your right hand.

Note the dew pond in the field on your left. In limestone country rainwater rapidly disappears into the porous soil, and in order to retain moisture it is necessary to dig out hollows and line them with a non-porous material. In the past this was usually clay, brought up from the valleys; today concrete or even plastic is used. These dew ponds have been constructed in this way since at least the middle ages, and many actually date from that time.

- At the far end of the field re-enter the enclosed green lane and keep ahead. Follow the lane through a gate and continue, now descending.
- At the bottom of the lane go through a gate onto the Monsal Trail and turn right.

The Monsal Trail is a long distance path/cycle route which follows the course of the Midlands Railway, built in the 1860s to connect Manchester with the east of the country at Buxton. The line was closed in 1967.

● Continue along the Monsal Trail for one-and-a quarter miles. Eventually pass a car-scrap yard on your right and then industrial units, to reach the renovated Bakewell Station buildings, just before a bridge over the trail.

When plans were made to build the Bakewell to Rowsley section of the Midland Railway in 1862, the Duke of Rutland objected that the line would pass too close to Haddon Hall and cause a nuisance (ignoring the detail that the Hall had been unoccupied for two hundred years and that his Lordship lived in Belvoir Castle, many miles away). Rutland had the power to insist that the line be built on higher ground, away from Haddon Hall, necessitating a costly tunnel and meaning that when the line reached Bakewell it would not be able to come into a station in the town centre but one would have to be built here on the hillside above.

● Turn right down the side of the Station Building, and cross the car park to the road.

● Turn left and follow the road as it curves right and descends.

The insistence of the Duke of Rutland that the railway line did not go near his deserted hall at Haddon forced users of the railway to have this long and steep walk between town and station every day.

● Near the bottom of the hill the road curves sharp right.

On the hill to your right was the site of Bakewell Castle. There was originally an Iron Age fort upon this site, built by one of the tribes in the Brigantean federation (see walks 4 and 5). It was surrounded by a strong ditch and an embankment, and unusually topped with a wall made of stone, a sign of its strategic importance in unsettled times. Edward the Elder built a fortress or 'Burgh' on this site in 920AD, part of his policy of consolidating the expanding influence of Wessex with a string of fortifications. It was in this burgh that the Conference of Bakewell took place, which effectively united all of England under Edward's rule.

● The car park is at the bottom of the hill.

Walk 9

Peveril Castle: the Norman Conquest of the north

Distance: 4.5 miles

Map: OS sheet 110

Start and parking: pay & display car park in Castleton (grid ref: 149830) Castleton is on the A625, between Sheffield and Chapel-en-le-Frith, at the foot of Winnats Pass.

Refreshments: Shops, tearooms and public houses in Castleton.

Historical Background

Three years after the Normans defeated King Harold at Hastings, the hill country of northern Derbyshire was the scene of continued resistance to William the Conqueror. It was a sanctuary for fleeing rebels, who were aided by a Danish army which landed in the Humber. William sent a considerable army northwards in 1069-70, to subjugate the area, and maybe as many as 100,000 people were put to death across northern England. Huge areas of the Peak forcibly depopulated, hastening the trend already present for the population to abandon the marginal lands of the hills for the more easily worked lowlands. An 80 square mile area of the Peak and a smaller area in the Derwent valley were designated as Royal Forests, reserved for the Kings private hunting. William Peveril, the Conquerors illegitimate son, was appointed Steward of the Royal Forest, and made Kings bailiff for Hope, Bakewell and Ashford

Part of King William's policy was to overawe the local conquered population with a show of strength, and massive castles were built to be a permanent reminder of Norman might. It was also policy to give the lands of the defeated Saxon aristocracy to his loyal Norman followers, thereby giving them a stake in securing the country. In line with this William Peveril was given a dozen manors, previously owned by local Saxons. With the revenue from these he built the strong and prominent fortress which now bears his name, from which to administer his new domains and to protect access to the valuable lead mining resources of the area. He also built a new town, Castleton, totally dependant upon the castle for its existence. It had a sturdy Norman church and the licence for the only market in the vicinity, both vehicles for further cementing the normanisation of the area. By 1086, at the time of the Doomsday Book, both castle and town were well established.

The Royal Forest and the vast estates of William Peveril formed a strategic buffer zone between the wild and lawless Pennines and Cumbria, and the more civilised and normanised south. Wolves, wild boar and deer were hunted by the King and his supporters amongst the forests and dales of the Peak. Lead continued to be mined in greater volumes than before to meet the demands generated by the upsurge in new castles and cathedrals. A few Normanised towns such as Castleton and Bakewell started to flourish. But 50 previously rich manors in the Peak were now dismissed in the Doomsday Book with the sinister entry 'It is waste', and it was not until many years after the Conquest before the Peak rebuilt its former affluence.

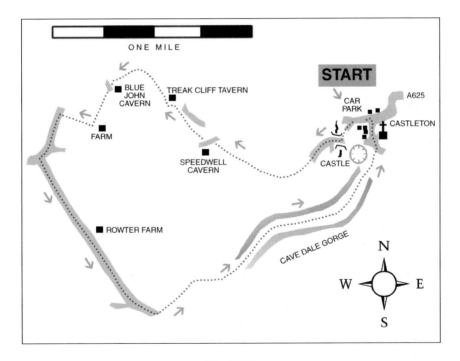

The Walk

This walk starts in Castleton and climbs out of the Hope valley, affording excellent views. It passes several caverns open to the public, before crossing open moor and returning down the spectacular Cave Dale Gorge to Peveril Castle.

● From the car park return to the main road.

- Cross the road at the mini-roundabout and bear half-right up the lane opposite, signed 'Riverside walk to Peak Cavern'.
- In 30 yards the lane narrows to an alleyway between houses. Keep straight on, with the river on your right.
- Follow the alley out to a lane. Turn right, crossing a bridge in 10 yards.

The Peak Cavern has one of the most spectacular entrances to any cave in Britain, a monumental gash 100 foot wide and 60 feet high in the vertical limestone cliffs. The entrance was used for centuries by rope makers who lived in the cave, and their homes and machinery can still be seen, as well as touring the galleries and underground rivers of the cave complex.

The entrance is a short detour up the path. Open daily 10am-6pm, entrance fee.

- For the main walk DO NOT turn right towards Peak Cavern but keep straight ahead up the lane (Goosehill).
- At a fork in 75 yards, keep straight on. The lane shortly becomes a stony path. Keep on up the path, still climbing.
- After 100 yards follow the path through a gate onto the moor. Keep ahead along the path, with a wall on your right.
- Curve right with the path and wall to reach a gate.
- Go through the gate and keep ahead, still with a wall on the right.
- When the wall drops away to the right, keep ahead along a clear path around the side of the hill.
- Cross a step stile by a gate, to emerge in a lane at the entrance to Speedwell Cavern.

Mining for galena or lead ore was a major industry in the Castleton area for 2,000 years. Speedwell Cavern is one of several old lead mines in the area now open to the public. Its major attraction is one particular tunnel or 'level', which took 11 years to dig in a fruitless search for veins of lead, 200 years ago. The level is now flooded and access for visitors is by boat. At the end of the level is the so-called Bottomless Pit, a huge pit down which the miners dumped the waste rock. Emptying over 40,000 tons of rubble into the pit made no appreciable difference to its depth.

The mine was closed at the end of the last century as uneconomic.

Open daily 10am-6pm, entrance fee.

- Cross the lane half-left to cross a step stile by a gate opposite.
- Continue straight on. In 30 yards cross a track. DO NOT go downhill with the track but continue straight on around the slope on an indistinct path, to reach a step stile over a wall.
- Cross the stile and continue around the bottom of the moor, with a wall and trees on your right.

Peveril Castle.

● After the trees end, follow a tumble-down wall around the slope, to reach a concrete path, high above the road.

● Turn left up the path, soon to reach the entrance to Treak Cliff Cavern.
This cavern was never a lead mine but is a natural cave in the limestone, discovered in the early years of this century. They contain a magnificent collection of stalagmites and stalactites, mineral pillars created by water dripping through limestone. There

was also limited mining for 'Blue John' or fluorite here from at least 1762, when Blue John from this cavern was used in making a decorative fireplace in Kedleston Hall, Derby. Extraction of Blue John continued until the end of the first world war, when it was used as a flux, or cleansing agent, in blast furnaces. In 1926 blasting extended the cavern to include the natural cave seen today.

Open daily 10am-6pm, entrance fee.

● Climb steps to the left of the cavern tearooms. At the top of the steps turn right along 'Public Footpath'.

● Cross a stile and follow the clear path around open hillside. Follow the path as it curves left, climbing all the time.

From this path there are magnificent views back down the valley over Castleton and beyond, somewhat marred by the concrete works at Hope. The pointed peak of Win Hill is clearly distinguishable on the horizon.

● Bend sharp left with the path up the side of a dry valley, to reach a stile on the skyline.

● Cross the stile and keep straight on across open moor on an indistinct path.

The huge bulk of Mam Tor looms up on your right. 1695 feet high, it marks the end of the limestone uplands of the Peaks and the beginning of the shales and gritstones of the Pennines. At some point in its history the steepness of the mountain and the shaley nature of its rock has caused a huge section of the slope to fall away, creating the distinctive shape we see today. Landslips still occur at intervals on Mam Tor, giving rise to its local name, 'The Shivering Mountain'. On the summit of Mam Tor are the clear remains of a hill fort, originally thought to be Iron Age but now identified as being from the earlier Bronze Age (see walk 4).

● Soon the roof of the entrance to Blue John Cavern is seen ahead.

● Cross the stile by a gate onto the entrance drive to Blue John Cavern. Turn left to pass the entrance.

'Blue John' or fluorite is a common mineral and the ore extracted from it, fluorite, has been mined in this area for centuries. It is only in the Blue John cavern that it is found in blue and yellow bands, much prized for making jewellery and ornaments. As well as several spectacular mineral caverns, the cavern also houses a museum of mining tools.

Open daily 10am-6pm, entrance fee.

● Pass the entrance on your left and cross a stile at the end of a small parking area.

● Continue ahead up the slope along an indistinct path, with the road away to your right.

● Curve left around the slope, climbing steadily. Soon the roof of a farm comes into sight ahead.

● Aim 100 yards to the right of the farm, to cross a stile.

- Keep ahead across the field, aiming for a stile beside a National Trust sign. Cross the stile onto a road.

- Turn left up the road. In 200 yards pass a side road leading to 'Castleton Caverns and Peveril Castle'.

- In a further 40 yards pass a ladder stile on your left. Keep going up the road for a further 20 yards, then turn left through a gate, to 'Rowter Farm'.

- Go up this minor tarmaced road, walled on your left, for half a mile, to pass the entrance to Rowter Farm.

- Keep straight on, still with the wall on your left, along a now less well-surfaced track.

- At a gateway, ignore a ladder-stile on the left signposted to 'Castleton'. Pass through the gate and keep straight on down the track, now enclosed.

- After a further half a mile, at a T-junction with another track, turn left.

- 300 yards later, cross a ladder stile by a gate and immediately turn left through a gate, marked with a blue 'bridleway' arrow.

- 20 yards later go through a second gate and then bear half-left across the field. (The distinctive cone of Win Hill is straight ahead of you.)

- Level with a quarry away to the right, the track descends into a dip. DO NOT go straight ahead to climb out of the dip on the other side along the bridleway. Instead turn right down the gully and make for a pedestrian gate in a wall 50 yards ahead.

- Go through the gate and continue ahead on a clear path down the gully.

- Go through another pedestrian gate and curve left, following the wall on your left hand.

- Where the wall swings left away from the path and starts to climb, DO NOT follow the broad path alongside it but turn right down the ever-deepening gully.

- Pass between gate posts and continue down the narrow dry valley.

- Go through another gate and plunge down the spectacular Cave Dale Gorge. Peveril Castle stands on the crags high above you.

Where the castle keep stands, the gorge is 45 feet wide and 230 feet deep. It was created when part of the cavern system that riddles these hills collapsed. The keep is visible on top of the cliffs to your left, and the body of the castle, the great hall and castle buildings, are behind it. The outer bailey, and main entrance were on the plateau to the right of the gorge, and entrance to the castle was across a narrow fixed wooden bridge that crossed this fearsome natural moat.

- Descend with care the steep and stony path (which can be slippery in wet weather) passing beneath Peveril Castle.

- Follow the gorge down to a stile and gate, leading into a footpath. Follow the footpath out to a road.

- Turn left and follow the road downhill, passing the village green with its memorials to two World Wars on your right.

Castleton did not grow organically but was laid down in a deliberate grid pattern, built at the same time as the castle by William Peveril, Steward of the Royal Forest of the Peak. The church of St Edmund's was built in the centre, with the market square(now somewhat encroached upon) to its south, with a defensive bank and ditch surrounding the town. The town was built with the deliberate intention of attracting traders and craftsmen who would bring an income in rents and market fees. Both as the major market in the area, actively supported by the Norman ruler of the lands, and as the location of the foremost Norman church, Castleton rapidly flourished and played a major role in introducing Norman culture to the area.

- To visit the castle, turn left in front of the Youth Hostel.

Peveril Castle was one of several castles built by William Peveril to defend his fiefdom in Derbyshire and Nottinghamshire. Most of these castles were only temporary affairs, rapidly constructed of earth and wood. This area was a political backwater to the normans, and once the immediate threat of rebellion had been suppressed, most of the castles were allowed to fall into disuse. The exception was the castle here, which William Peveril made into his administrative centre.

Peveril Castle was built on a triangular spur, protected by Peak Cavern Gorge on the south-west and Cave Dale to the south-east. On the far side of Cave Dale was the outer bailey and original castle entrance, with access to the castle proper over an easily defended wooden bridge. The third, northern side, has a steep slope down into the town and was topped by a sturdy curtain wall, built around 1080AD. The foundations of this wall are the oldest part of the castle still visible, seen beneath a flimsier, more modern wall. The only entrance into the castle today is up a steep zig-zag path to what was the rear entrance to the castle, a gatehouse built into the curtain wall. This provides a splendid vantage point from which to view the planned town of Castleton and the strategic position of the castle above the Hope Valley. Within the curtain wall, on the summit of the triangular spur, was the inner bailey, containing the Hall, Chapel, domestic rooms and massive Keep, the last line of defence for the castle in the event of attack.

By the time of his death William Peveril had accumulated an extensive estate in the county of Derbyshire, which he passed on to his son, William. This latter William supported King Stephen in the civil wars and in 1155 forfited his estates and the Castle to Henry II, who extended the castles defences and built the massive keep. Peveril became a royal castle, managed by a royal constable.

The only action seen by the castle was in 1215, when the constable sided with the Barons in their revolt against King John. The Kings supporter the Earl of Derby, made half-hearted threats to take the castle by force of arms, but the situation was resolved by the Kings death and no major siege was forthcoming.

Despite being given briefly to Simon de Montfort in 1254 by Henry III, and by Edward II to his lover Piers Gaveston in 1308, the castle remained royal property until 1369, when Edward III gave it to his cousin John of Gaunt, Duke of Lancaster. Thus the castle became part of the Duchy of Lancaster and served as the headquarters of the Duchy's Peak estates, before falling into disuse and ruin in the sixteenth century.

Open Easter to 31 October, daily 10am-6pm; 1 November to Easter, Wednesday-Sunday 10am-4pm. Entrance fee, free to members of English Heritage.

● To return to the car park, turn right in front of the Youth Hostel and follow Castle Street past the church on the right and a row of pubs, tearooms and B&Bs on the left, to reach the main road.

● Turn left along the main road back to the car park.

Walk 10

Chelmorton: villages and fields in the middle ages

Distance: 5 miles

Map: OS sheet 119

Start and parking: The walk starts from the Wye Dale car park on the A6, three miles east of Buxton (grid ref: 104725).

Refreshments: None.

Historical Background

The fertile valleys of the Trent and the lower Derwent, had been settled since pre-Roman times. By the time the Normans came to impose their rule on the area, successive migrations by both the Anglo-Saxons and the Danes had dramatically increased the population of Derbyshire's southern lowlands. Northern and western Derbyshire, especially the area of the White Peak, remained comparatively sparsely populated, and indeed suffered an initial decrease in population following the rebellion of 1069-70 (see walk 9). During the next century active steps were taken to re-populate the area which had been declared a wasteland in the Domesday Book. Southern monasteries were given vast grants of land on condition that they turned to sheep-rearing, to produce the wool necessary for England's growing textile trade. In addition, pioneer farmers were encouraged to resettle the Peak with the promise of land, and villages were allowed to expand unchecked.

The traditional view of the middle ages is of peasants feudally bound to the land of their lords. This was broadly correct in southern and eastern England, the areas most exposed to Norman feudalism, but it was not universal across the whole country. In the areas settled by the Danes, including Derbyshire, it was more usual for farmers to be free men, paying a monthly rent to a lord but retaining personal freedom over their lives and their land. On the Peak, ancient British in culture until comparatively late, the old tendency towards free farmers still prevailed. Both these traditions mitigated against any extensive normanisation of Derbyshire.

Although the farmers of Derbyshire may have had more freedom than their southern counterparts, they shared the same agricultural practices. Cultivation took place in two, or more rarely, three huge open fields surrounding a village, with each villager owning a number of strips within each field. This open field system meant that every operation must be conducted in common by all villagers, and no one could produce crops at a different time or that required different treatment to his neighbours. This led to great conservatism in farming methods.

Changes in agricultural practice from the sixteenth century onwards led to the disappearance of the open fields, and increasing prosperity changed the medieval village beyond recognition. On the poor agricultural land of the Peak, it is still possible to see examples of medieval village life. One such example is at Chelmorton.

The Walk

This walk crosses open fields and moorland to visit Chelmorton, a village and surrounding fields whose layout is virtually unchanged since the middle Ages, before returning down the spectacular gorge of Deep Dale.

● From the car park cross the busy A6 and go up an enclosed footpath to the left of the access road to the quarry opposite. The path follows an enclosed water channel.

● A few yards after passing the end of the water channel, at a fork, take the left fork, signed 'Chelmorton'.

● Follow the footpath up a dry valley, which ends in a 'churn hole'.

A 'churn hole' is a natural pothole, caused by water seeping through the cracks in the porous limestone and eroding it away. Over the centuries the hole gets deeper, water flows into it more rapidly, and swirls or 'churns' around in the bottom, eventually wearing the rock away to form a cave. This cave was used in the iron age as a shelter from the elements, and a bronze pin from that period was found here.

● Go up the slope to the right of the churn hole and climb steeply out of the valley to a stile.

● Cross the stile onto a moor and keep ahead, with the wall on your left hand.

● At a tumbled-down cross wall go ahead through a squeeze stile and keep straight on, with the wall still on your left. Where the wall turns left, keep straight on, aiming for a stile in the top right-hand corner of the field.

● Cross the stile and keep straight on for 30 yards to pass through a gap in the wall. Maintain your line of advance, following the wall on your right hand to a stile.

● Cross the stile and keep ahead to a gate opposite, passing a farm on your right.

● Go through the gate and go straight on to a metal field gate, giving access to a green lane.

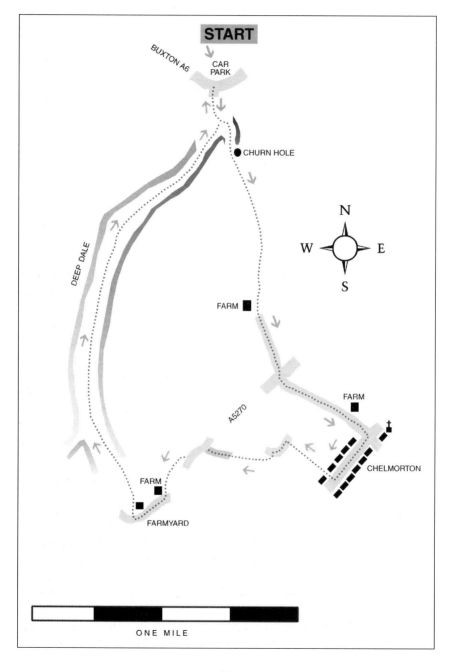

START

BUXTON A6

CAR PARK

CHURN HOLE

DEEP DALE

N

W

E

S

FARM

FARM

A5270

FARM

CHELMORTON

FARMYARD

ONE MILE

- Go along the green lane and then keep ahead in the next field, with the wall on your left hand.
- Go through a gate and keep ahead, to go along the green lane ahead.
- Follow the green lane out to a road. cross the road and go along the lane opposite.
- At a T-junction in front of a farm, maintain your line of advance along the track towards the village.

To your right was one of the two huge open fields around Chelmorton. In addition, there would have been an area of common, uncultivated, land upon which the villagers could graze their animals, normally pigs.

The communal fields were divided into strips for ease of ploughing. Each villager would have owned one or more strips of land, scattered across each field to ensure that all villagers shared the good and the poor land. The length of each strip or 'furrow' was dictated in part by the lie of the land, but the breadth was always approximately 16.5 feet, the width that a team of eight oxen could conveniently plough. Gradually over time the length became a standardised 'furrow length' or 'furlong'. Ownership of a team of oxen was beyond the means of most villagers, so resources were pooled at ploughing time. As the ox plough moved along the furrow, it threw up the earth into a bank, and these banks gradually became the boundaries between neighbours. An additional, temporary, boundary would have been put up at the ends of each strip, to protect the crops from animals straying from the common grazing land. These needed to be temporary, so that they could be removed each ploughing time to allow the oxen to turn around and to move to the next strip.

As the ownership of a strip was passed down through the generations, the boundaries became more permanent, with stone walls eventually replacing the earthen banks and temporary fences. The pattern of long, thin, stone-walled fields you see on your right has not altered since the early middle ages. Whilst most open-field land was enclosed from Elizabethan times onwards, the land around Chelmorton was of such poor quality that enclosure was not worthwhile, and so the field pattern has remained untouched.

- Follow the track out to a road, and turn right down the main (and only) street in Chelmorton.

In southern England, the Lord lived on his manor, and the focal points of the village were the twin pillars of Norman feudalism, manor house and church. In the north, villages still had a pattern dating from Roman times, when the focal point was a farm, with the dwellings of relatively free workers in its vicinity. The landlord was a more remote figure, both before and after the Conquest, and villages did not therefore cluster around a manor house. The layout of Chelmorton is unaltered since those days.

Chelmorton had a constant spring providing fresh water, which surfaced above the church and fed a stream running downhill. The only street in Chelmorton followed the stream, with the houses in a line along the street, and their yards backing onto the open fields on either side of the village. The bulk of the population were free men, who owned a cottage and some land, between one and five acres. They grew vegetables and kept hens in the plot of land at the back of their cottage. They may have owned the odd pig, which would have been grazed upon the common land attached to the village in summer. The two huge fields around the village were used to cultivate cereals, to produce grain for gruel, bread and beer, and also to provide winter fodder for those animals not slaughtered.

● Pass 'The Smithy' on your right (*a reminder that some villagers had specialist skills within the community*) and shortly after pass an unusual stone built, green-doored telephone box. Eighty yards later, turn right at a footpath sign.

● Go along a concrete drive and through a gate. Keep ahead for 10 yards. Do not turn right with the drive but keep straight on through a white gate, along the back of a house and over a stile into a field.

● Keep straight on, with the wall on your right, to a stile. Cross the stile and keep ahead for the next two fields, the wall now on your left.

This field is the typical narrow strip, unaltered in size and shape since medieval days but simply enclosed with stone walls.

● At the end of the field, leave by a stile beside a gate, into a green lane. Turn left down the lane.

● Follow the lane around a right-hand turn, but then immediately cross a stile on the left.

● Go half-right across the field, aiming for a gateway just to the left of a metal field gate.

● Go through the gateway and go along a green lane. After 100 yards do not turn into a field but keep ahead along a continuation of the lane.

These green lanes follow the route of old medieval lanes, which ran across the open fields, between the strips of land cultivated by individual villagers, giving access to various groups of strips.

● Follow the green lane out to a road, and turn left along the road.

● Where the road bends left, turn right over a wooden stile and 5 yards later cross the wall by a ladder stile into a field.

● Go quarter left across the field, aiming just to the right of telegraph poles. Soon a gate comes into sight more or less ahead.

● Cross a stile 15 yards to the left of the gate and go along the field ahead, with the wall on your left hand, to cross a stile on the far side, giving access onto a road.

● Turn right down the road for 250 yards. Where the road bends sharp right, turn right at a bridleway sign, through a pedestrian gate into a farmyard.

Fields at Chelmorton, still showing mediaeval strips.

● Go down the farmyards and out via a metal field gate.

● Keep ahead down Horseshoe Dale, curving left and then right with the dale, descending all the time. The dale soon becomes gorge-like.

● After half a mile, Back Dale joins from the left. Bear right into what is now Deep Dale and continue down the sheer-sided gorge.

● In half a mile, where a path crosses the stream and a stile to the left, keep straight on down the gorge, following the stream.

● In another half a mile, at the end of the valley, cross a stile and keep straight on along a track, follow the track along the side of a blasting area.

● The track narrows into a footpath. Continue straight on, descending steeply into the valley.

● Cross a stile and turn left into a footpath, soon enclosed. Follow this footpath and retrace your outward steps back to the A6 and the car park opposite.

Haddon Hall and the Kings of the Peak

Distance: 5.5 miles

Map: OS sheet 119

Start and parking: There are a number of car parks in Bakewell, all pay & display. It is recommended that you park in the long stay car park, which is at the far end of the town bridge, where the A619 and the B6408 meet before entering Bakewell. Do not be confused that the car park is signed as both 'car park' and 'industrial estate'. The walk starts from the edge of the car park (grid ref: 220686.)

Refreshments: Shops, tearooms and public houses in Bakewell.

Historical Background

For almost eight hundred years Haddon Hall has been in the hands of two families, the Vernons and the Manners, great powers in their own locality but content to play little part in the wider, national political or social scene.

Richard Vernon acquired Haddon Hall in 1139, and it remained in the Vernon family for the next four centuries. The Vernons concentrated their attentions upon their Derbyshire estates. Over successive generations they acquired large amounts of land, bought piecemeal and then enclosed, for sheep rearing and for timber. They bought into local leadmining and developed the industry considerably. They became major property owners in nearby towns, notably Bakewell. In the process they came to have a total control over the economic and political life of this part of Derbyshire, and in the sixteenth century the autocratic manners of George Vernon led to him becoming known as the 'King of the Peak'.

According to legend, it was in 1547 that Dorothy Vernon ignored the wishes of George Vernon, her staunchly Catholic father, and eloped from Haddon Hall at dead of night with Sir John Manners, the son of a family of rich but protestant landowners. The Manners family had acquired a considerable fortune in land, and were the only rivals to the Vernons as a local power. Whatever the truth behind the story, the marriage of Dorothy and John united the two most powerful local families. Ten years later the Haddon Estates passed into the Manners' family.

The uniting of these two great holdings made the Manners the pre-eminent family in the Peak District, rulers in fact if not in law. In 1641 a later John Manners was created Earl of Rutland. The family were staunch parliamentarians, and in the Civil War used their influence over the predominantly royalist district to keep the Peak neutral. Gradually over the next half century the family moved its interests to their new home at Belvoir Castle, leaving Haddon deserted. Their involvement with the Peak continued however, with the family exercising their power to influence railway construction, forest planting and land development. In 1800, the now-Duke of Rutland, seeing the success of nearby Buxton (see walk 23) started to develop Bakewell as a spa town (see walk 8). Although some building took place the plans never came to fruition.

The Walk

This walk starts in Bakewell and follows the River Wye to Haddon Hall, before returning across fields and moor to Bakewell again.

● Leave the long stay car park and make your way to the old town bridge, which carries the main road (A619) into Bakewell.

Although the original town bridge was widened in the nineteenth century, its mediaeval structure can still be seen. It was built to be wide enough for a laden horse-drawn cart to cross, with alcoves for pedestrians to shelter in to avoid being crushed.

● Cross over the busy bridge with care, staying on the narrow left hand pavement. Immediately at the end of the bridge, turn sharp left down to reach the river bank. Here turn right and walk downstream, with the river on your left hand.

● Ignore footbridges and keep ahead into the recreation field. Keep along the river bank, passing behind the cricket pavilion.

● Stay on the tarmaced path as it leaves the river bank and curves around the football pitch. At the railings around a children's playground, turn left down an alley between houses.

● At the end of the alley cross slightly right over the road and continue down the alley opposite.

● Follow the alley out to a road and turn left to cross a road bridge over the River Wye.

● At the far end of the bridge keep ahead along the road for 100 yards, to the metal entrance gates to the 'Agricultural Business Centre'. Go through the gates with the road but immediately turn half-right and make for a stile in the corner of the field.

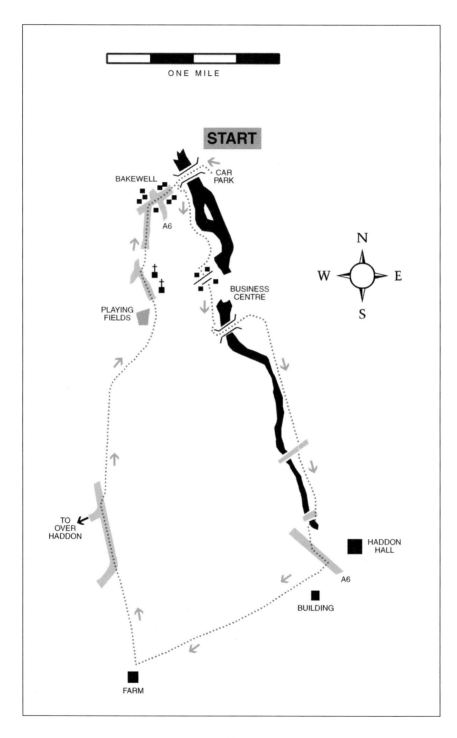

- Cross the stile and follow the left-hand edge of a large field. Where the river meets the path, keep ahead, still with a hedge on your left.

- In the bottom corner of the field, where the hedge meets the river, cross a small stream via a plank footbridge and keep ahead into woods, now with the river close on your right hand.

- Cross a stile and keep straight on along the bottom of a field, still on the river bank.

- Climb a bank and continue straight on along a well-defined track, initially along the river bank but then across a meadow, to reach a gate onto a track.

- Turn right down the track for 15 yards, then turn left onto a footpath along the river bank.

- Follow the path for 500 yards to a stone footbridge over the River Wye.

- Follow an enclosed footpath out to the A6.

- Turn left and walk down the A6 for 200 yards to reach Haddon Hall.

Look out for a milestone a hundred yards down the road on the opposite side. This was on the old turnpike, and shows 150 miles to London.

- Opposite the gates to Haddon Hall, cross the road to take a footpath at a sign opposite, just on the Bakewell side of the Haddon Hall car park.

Haddon Hall is the most perfectly preserved mediaeval manor house in the Derbyshire, and indeed one of the best in all England. Although it developed continually as a building from the eleventh to the seventeenth centuries, it then stood deserted and untouched for 200 years.

The original building was a manor house, built by William Peveril (see walk 9), as a retreat from the pressures of state. It served as private palace and as hunting lodge, surrounded as it was by the rich hunting grounds of the Royal Forest of the Peak, of which Peveril was Warden. Although a strong tower, the Peveril Tower, was added soon after its construction, this was more for prestige than for any defensive necessity. Today only the tower and the chapel remain of that original Norman manor. Peveril's son, also William, supported King Stephen in the civil wars of the twelfth century, and in 1155 forfeited his estates to the new king, Henry II. Haddon passed to his tenant, William Avenel and hence to the latter's son-in-law Richard Vernon in 1179.

After Richard Vernon acquired Haddon he built a twelve foot high wall around the house, later with battlements added for decoration. The wall would have kept out thieves, or protected the manor from discontented peasants, but was not designed to withstand any determined military assault. Later generations of Vernons added a cross-wing in the fourteenth century, battlements in the fifteenth century, and a gatehouse and courtyard in the sixteenth century. The Vernons shared their predecessors love of hunting, and an enclosed deerpark was built surrounding the Hall.

Under the Manners family, from 1567 onwards, the Hall was further extended, primarily with the introduction of a minstrel gallery and splendid terraced gardens, which originally included a bowling green. The surrounding deer park, in keeping with current fashion, started to be landscaped in the early eighteenth century into a formal park. This project was never completed, as by then the Manners' attention was turning elsewhere.

After the Civil War had ended in 1649, the Manners Family were Earls of Rutland, later to become Dukes. Gradually over the next half century the family moved its interests to their new home at Belvoir Castle in Leicestershire, and Haddon Hall was left empty, although meticulously maintained. It thus escaped any of the changing architectural fashions of the eighteenth and nineteenth centuries. In the early twentieth century the 9th Duke, then Marquis of Granby, set about restoring the Hall, preserving as much of the original fabric as possible, and where necessary making replacement in the original style.

Today the house is acclaimed as one of the most romantic buildings in Britain and is a perfect example of a mediaeval manor house.

Open daily April to September, 11.00am-5.00pm. Entrance charge.

- Walk away from the A6, with the car park on your left, and go through a field gate.
- Keep straight on up the edge of a field, with a wall on your right and a disused building off to your left.

You soon pass a walled enclosure on the left, a brief way up the slope. This contains a dew pond, an artificial depression in the limestone, lined with non-porous clay, in which to collect rainwater for watering stock.

There are fine views back to Haddon Hall, nestling in the trees on the opposite side of the valley.

- Pass through a gate and continue ahead, now with the wall on your left.
- At the top of the field, pass through a pedestrian gate beside a field gate, and keep straight on, still with a wall on your left.
- At the end of the next field, follow the wall around to the right for 10 yards to cross a stile by a gate.
- Continue the same line of advance, still with a wall on the left, towards a farm and barn seen in the distance.
- Continue to the corner of the field, with the barn on the left. Here turn sharp right and walk up the field, with a wall on your left.
- Cross a stile by a gate and continue ahead along a track up the side of a field, still with a wall on the left.
- Follow the track to a gate and out onto a lane.
- Keep straight on down the lane. Pass a farm on the right and a turning to Over Haddon on the left.

- 150 yards later, turn right at a footpath sign and go through a pedestrian gate. DO NOT go straight down the field, but instead go half-left across the field.

- Go through a stile and continue in the same direction across the next field. Pass under telephone wires and make for a stile in the wall on the right.

- Cross the stile and go half-left down the next field. Go through a gate at the bottom of the dip.

- Continue ahead along a narrow field, and exit in the far left corner through a field gate.

- Continue along the bottom of a field, in a depression with a wall on your right.

- Go between stone gateposts and continue ahead along an enclosed track, narrowing once past a metal squeeze stile.

- Leave the enclosed path and continue ahead, still with the wall on your right.

- Pass through two squeeze stiles and walk along the bottom of playing fields, behind a fence on your left.

- Join a drive and continue along it to a road.

- Keep straight on down the road, passing beside two churches and a cemetery on your right.

- At the end of the road, turn right past the gates of the cemetery. Beside a letter box, turn right down a wide, handrailed, tarmaced pathway.

- Follow the path as it winds down into town, ignoring footpaths off to the sides. The path eventually becomes a residential road. Keep straight on.

The road you are walking down is called Butts Road, a name that indicates the roads mediaeval past. In the middle of the fourteenth century, under the demands of the Hundred Years War, England had developed a weapon which was to dominate the battlefields of Europe for 200 years, namely the longbow. In skilled hands this weapon could drive a metal tipped arrow through the thickest armour at a range of 250 yards. To ensure this skill existed a form a military service was introduced: every commoner was required on pain of fines to practice with the longbow for two hours every week, after the Sunday church service was finished. An area was set aside for this practice, usually waste ground abutting the town walls, and named the after the straw targets used, known as 'butts'.

- Pass Bakewell Working Mens Club on your right and follow the road out to a more major road, where turn right opposite the St Johns Alms Houses.

The original St Johns Hospital was built on this site in 1602. Not a 'hospital' in todays sense of the word, but rather a 'hospice'. The building was to provide accommodation in a barrack-like building for six 'worthy poor' old men of the borough, who lived in spartan conditions under an almost military regime and were required to wear a uniform – a gown with the blue and yellow cross of St John on the

Haddon Hall.

breast – in return for the charity they received. The original hospital was pulled down in 1709 and six almshouses erected in its place, which provided private dwellings for the poor. The building is still used as an almshouse, although now it has been modernised into three homes.

- Keep straight on, passing the Rutland Arms Hotel on your left.

- Cross the A6-Matlock Road at the pedestrian crossing, and then resume the same line advance walk down the right hand side of Rutland Square.

- Pass the old Market Hall, now housing the Tourist Information Centre, on your right.

- Keep ahead, along Bridge Street to the bridge. Cross over and back to the car park.

Wingfield Manor: Plantagenet Manor to Stuart Observatory

Distance: 5 miles

Map: OS sheet 119

Start and parking: The walk starts from the village centre of Crich, a triangle where the B5035 meets a minor road, in front of the Baptist Chapel (grid ref: 350542). Crich is on the B5042, five miles west of Alfreton, and two miles east of the A6 below Matlock.

Refreshments: Shops, tearoom and public houses in Crich, public houses in South Wingfield.

Historical Background

Wingfield Manor owes its existence to Ralph, Lord Cromwell, one of the most powerful men in fifteenth century England. He was one of the group of wild young men who were companions to Prince Hal, later Henry V, during the reign of Henry IV. Cromwell accompanied Henry V into France, fought with distinction at Agincourt, and was one of the four knights entrusted with bringing the king's body home to England after his premature death in 1422. Cromwell was appointed Chancellor to the infant King Henry VI, and was soon effectively one of the real rulers of England. Cromwell had the acumen to stand clear of the political in-fighting around the throne, that marred Henry VI's reign and culminated in the Wars of the Roses.

Cromwell, whose family home was at Tattershall Castle, in Lincolnshire, was a fanatical huntsman In order to be convenient for the Royal Forest of Duffield Frith, he acquired the manor of South Wingfield in 1429, after bitter legal wrangling with a rival claimant. A small, ruinous twelfth century castle which stood on the site was converted into a hunting lodge, which soon grew into a splendid and spacious palace, where Cromwell held court over his new estates as well as entertaining and relaxing.

Cromwell died without heirs in 1456, and his land passed into the hands of the Earls of Shrewsbury. The 6th Earl was appointed gaoler to Mary, Queen of Scots in 1567, and kept her in a number of his Derbyshire properties. The queen was twice lodged in Wingfield Manor, in 1569 and again in 1584. It was during the latter visit that one of Shrewsbury's attendants, Anthony Babington, developed his infatuation with the Queen, allegedly visiting her disguised as a gypsy, and later developing the harebrained plan for her rescue that resulted in both their deaths (see walk 14).

During the Civil War, Wingfield Manor was held by both royalists and parliament at various times. After the war its defences were slighted to stop it ever again being used as a military base. With the Restoration of the monarchy in 1660 Wingfield Manor was sold to the Halton family, who restored part of the manor as a residence. The new king, Charles II, was keen supporter of science, establishing the Royal Society of which a later Halton, Immanuel, was a member. Immanuel was a keen astronomer and converted the great hall into an observatory from which to study solar eclipses. The Haltons eventually moved out and Wingfield Manor became the farm it is today.

The Walk

This walk crosses pleasant rural countryside between Crich and South Wingfield, to pass the ruins of Wingfield Manor.

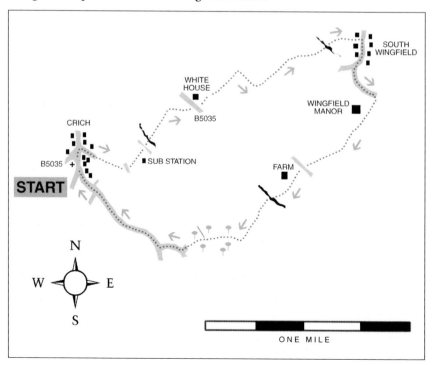

Wingfield Manor.

● Standing with your back to the Baptist Chapel, cross the road and go down School Lane, with the store to the left of the road entrance, and a butchers and a chip shop to the right.

● Pass the gates of Wylan Cottage on your right, and keep ahead, soon with school railings on your left hand, along an enclosed footpath.

● At the end of the enclosed footpath keep straight on, passing a house on your right-hand, to a stile into a field.

● Cross the stile and keep straight on down the long, narrowing, field, to reach a tarmaced drive. Turn half-left across the drive to a stile beside the left-most of two field gates.

● Cross the stile and keep ahead, initially with a hedge on your right hand, to a stile straight ahead.

● Cross the stile and keep straight ahead across the field.

To your left is the monument to the men of the Sherwood Foresters (the Nottingham and Derbyshire Regiment) on top of Crich Stand, 950 feet above sea level. Three beacon towers have stood on top of the limestone ridge above Crich: each has been destroyed by lightning. The present 63 foot high tower was erected in 1923 as a memorial to the men who died in World War One. It still has a revolving beacon light, lit at night and visible for miles.

● Pass to the left of a fenced electricity sub-station and keep straight on, with fence on your right hand, to reach a stile leading onto a quarry access road.

● Cross the road and cross a stile opposite. Proceed down the left-hand side of the field to a shallow stream.

● Cross the stream by stepping stones and climb the slope opposite to a metal field gate in front of you.

- Go through the gate and half-left across the field, to a squeeze stile in the top left-hand corner.
- Go through the stile and immediately turn right, to follow the hedge on your right hand up to a stone squeeze stile in the corner of the field.
- Go through the stile and turn left, to continue your line of advance, walking now with the hedge on your left to a stile in the corner of the field.
- Go through the stile and keep straight on, still with the hedge on your left, towards a white house seen ahead. Follow the hedge down to a gate and up the next field, still with the hedge on your left, to a stile by a gate.
- Go through the stile and keep ahead to a road (the B5035).
- Cross the road to a footpath post opposite. Go through the wall and up the slope. Keep ahead across the field, with telegraph wires some 15 yards to your left, to a squeeze stile.
- Go through the stile. Keep ahead for 10 yards to another stile giving onto a track.
- Turn left along the track for 15 yards, then turn right through a squeeze stile.
- Go quarter-left down the hill, passing between trees to reach a gateway, to the left of a farm.
- Go through the gate and keep straight on, with a wall on your left-hand. Follow the wall through two gates and across three narrow fields, to a stile in the corner of the third field.
- Cross the stile and maintain your line of advance across the next narrow field, to a squeeze stile.
- Go through the stile and turn right down the side of the field, with the wall on your right hand.
- After 50 yards, when you are half way down the field and opposite a telegraph pole, turn sharp left and go directly across the field, passing to the immediate right of the telegraph pole. Keep going along same line of advance to a squeeze stile in the middle of the hedge ahead.
- Go through the stile and keep straight on across the next field to a stile.

Wingfield Manor can be seen across the fields to your right. It occupies a good defensive site from which to dominate the surrounding landscape, and a small castle was built here in Norman times. By the time of Ralph, Lord Cromwell, three hundred years later, the strategic significance of the site had diminished, and a palace was built where the Norman castle had stood.

- Cross the stile and keep ahead, with a hedge on your left, to reach a stile in 80 yards.
- Cross this stile and keep straight on, with the hedge now on your right hand, down the field. Go through a gate and keep straight on, still with the hedge on your right, down the next field to a stile in the bottom corner.

- Cross the stile and keep straight on, the hedge still on your right, down a third field to a stile.

- Go over the stile and maintain your line of advance for five yards to a footbridge.

- Cross the footbridge and go half-right up the field, to a stile in the right-hand hedge.

- Cross the stile and keep ahead up a track between fences. The track becomes a fenced footpath which leads you around a house, and then is enclosed between a house and a fence, to reach the road in South Wingfield.

- Turn right down the hill, past the Old Yew Tree public house.

- Follow the road as it curves right. Fifty yards after the bend, turn left into the drive for Wingfield Manor (a sign saying 'No access' refers to cars, not pedestrians).

Although the walk goes most of the way around Wingfield Manor and passes close under its walls, there is no access to the Manor from this side. If you wish to visit the Manor you need to continue down this road for a third of a mile in the direction of Crich, and then turn up a drive on your left, signed 'South Wingfield Manor'.

Wingfield Manor is open April to November, Wednesday-Sunday noon-5pm; November, to March weekends only 10am-4pm. Admission charge, free to members of English Heritage.

- Follow the drive as it curves left, with Wingfield Manor on the hill to the right.

It can clearly be seen that Wingfield Manor was not built for defence. The buildings we can see were the Great Hall and to its right, the principal chambers of the building, built by Lord Cromwell between 1439 and 1456. The wings to either side have huge windows, providing a light and airy environment to live in, but defensively impractical. Wingfield Manor could be defended against roving bandits or if necessary the local peasantry, but it was not built to withstand determined assault by professional soldiers. It provided Cromwell with a pleasant home at which to entertain friends for hunting in the nearby forest. In times of major conflict, the castle at Tattershall would have become the family's military base. Lord Cromwell died before the Wars of the Roses started, and thus was not involved in that conflict.

- When the drive reaches twin gates, cross a stile beside the right hand gate and follow the track as it curves right and climbs, with the Manor still on your right.

- At the top of the slope, at a junction of paths, keep straight on uphill, up the track towards the Manor.

- Pass the gate into the farm on your right and keep ahead for 30 yards to a squeeze stile beside a farm gate.

The gate you have just passed on your right was the original entrance to the Manor, a stout gatehouse facing onto the ridge along which traffic would have approached. To the left of the gatehouse is a mediaeval tithe barn, constructed to hold the produce paid to Lord Cromwell as feudal rent by his retainers.

- Go through the stile and up the right hand side of a field to a stile by another gate.

- Go through the stile and then half-left along the top of the field, with a wall on your left hand.

Wingfield Manor saw action several times during the Civil War. By the sixteenth century gunpowder had taken over from the sword and the bow as the weapon of war, and the walls of the Manor, which would not been an ideal defence in the event of hand-to-hand fighting the previous century, now provided an excellent musket emplacement. At the beginning of the war the Manor was originally occupied by Parliamentarian forces, who were able to harass communications between the King's Oxford base and his northern troops. Eventually in November 1643 William Cavendish, Earl of Newcastle, commander of the Kings northern army, sallied forth from his base at Bolsover Castle (see walk 15) and besieged South Wingfield, but even with 500 men he was unable to dislodge the 40-man parliamentarian garrison. Eventually heavy artillery had to be brought up from Nottingham, probably placed upon the ridge where you are now standing. In 1643 this would have been open ground, with no hedges, trees or farm in the way, and the manor house was eventually battered into submission.

By the start of 1644 Parliamentary forces were making inroads into the Kings northern powerbase. The Earl of Newcastle retained a Royalist garrison in Wingfield, and used it as a forward base from which to harry the advancing Parliamentarian forces. Royal power in the north was broken after the battle of Marston Moor in July 1644, and the Earl of Newcastle fled to Holland. A strong Parliamentarian army recaptured Wingfield, and held the Manor for the rest of the War. At the end of the war the castle walls were slighted i.e. semi-demolished, to ensure they could never again be used to threaten the peace.

- At the corner of the field, DO NOT go straight on through the gate, but turn right down the same field, with the hedge on your left hand.

- Go through a gate and maintain your line of advance across the next field, aiming to the right of the farm seen ahead.

- Cross a stile on the far side of the field and descend to the road.

- Cross the road and go through the red metal gate opposite.

- DO NOT go along the metalled drive towards the farm, but follow the left hand edge of the field, keeping a hedge on your left. At the bottom of the field, the right of way is to keep straight on, crossing the tumble down wall at the point where a field gate leans upon it. (In practice, at the time of writing this was rather precarious, and it may be better to go through a gate in the hedge on your left, half way down the field, and walk down the opposite side of the hedge to rejoin the right of way on the other side of this wall).

- Continue your same line of advance down the next field, aiming for the bottom right-hand corner. Twenty yards short of the corner, turn right over a waymarked stile.
- From the stile, go half-left down the field to gates in the bottom corner.
- DO NOT go through the metal gate, but go through an open gateway just to its right. Cross the brook via a farm bridge, and follow the track as it curves right, uphill.
- In the top corner of the field, turn left through a squeeze stile by a gate.
- Keep ahead up the side of the field, with a wall on your right hand.
- In the top corner of the field, turn right for 10 yards to go through a gate, then turn left to continue your same line of advance, now with the wall on your left hand.
- At the top of the field go through a squeeze stile beside a gate, into a green lane. Turn right along the lane for 30 yards, to a stile by a metal field gate.
- Go through the stile and continue up the footpath beyond. In 20 yards ignore field gates to left and right, but keep ahead through a squeeze stile and up an enclosed footpath.
- Where the path ceases to be enclosed, keep ahead through a narrow wood, following the footpath as it curves left and then right. At the end of the band of trees, turn right beside a wall for five yards to a stile.
- Cross the stile and turn left along the bottom of a field, to enter woods again via a stile.
- Follow a clear path up through the woods for 100 yards to a T-junction, where turn left.
- Follow the path down through the woods, soon with a wall and fence on your right hand.
- Follow the path out into a field. Descend the field to a track and turn left down the track to a metal field gate.
- Go through the gate and turn right along a track. Pass houses on your right hand and go down to a T-junction, where turn right up a lane.
- Follow the lane for three-quarters of a mile, ignoring all side turnings.
- At a T-junction, turn right, to reach the centre of Crich and the Baptist Hall in 50 yards.

Hardwick Hall: the story of a Tudor courtier

Distance: 4.5 miles

Map: OS sheet 120

Start and parking: The walk starts from the Rowthorne Trail car park and picnic area, where there is free parking (grid ref: 476648). The car park is on a minor road just south of the village of Rowthorne, which itself is one mile south of Glapwell. Glapwell is on the A617, two miles west of Junction 29 of the M1, and four miles north-east of Mansfield.

Refreshments: None

Historical Background

Elizabeth, Countess of Salisbury, known universally as Bess of Hardwick, was one of the great figures of the Tudor era, who left a major mark upon her home county of Derbyshire. She was in disgrace during the reign of Mary Tudor for the support she and her husband gave to Princess Elizabeth. Bess was rewarded when Elizabeth came to the throne, and came as close as any woman did to being a friend of the Queen. In an age when marriage was seen as the only career for a woman, she became an influential and controversial figure at court in her own right. She married four times, her fortune increasing with each occasion, and became one of Derbyshire's greatest landowners.

Bess was born in 1518, the daughter of the de Harwicke family. These were minor gentry, who were left in financial difficulties when Bess's father died the year after she was born. Bess's first marriage at the age of twelve was to a boy one year her senior. It lasted only a year before her husband died, and she was almost immediately remarried to Sir William Cavendish, a major landowner in Derbyshire, a privy councillor and powerful courtier. During Mary Tudor's reign, Sir William was hounded to an early grave by Mary's supporters for his friendship with Princess Elizabeth, leaving Bess wealthy in land, including Chatsworth House. Her own friendship with Elizabeth gave her prominence in the new queen's court. Bess soon married Sir William St Loe, the ageing captain of the queen's guard who shortly died, leaving her another huge estate.

Bess's fourth marriage in 1567 was to George Talbot, Earl of Shrewsbury, one of the richest men in England with vast estates in Derbyshire and surrounding counties. Bess, rich and powerful and in her late forties, was not prepared to play the dutiful wife and the marriage gradually deteriorated, with public and acrimonious disagreements. Bess even went so far as to accuse her husband of having an affair with Mary, Queen of Scots, whose gaoler he was (see walks 12 and 14). Eventually the Queen herself was forced to intervene and demand the couple settle their differences. After a public show of reconciliation, the two led separate lives until Shrewsbury died in 1590.

Bess, now enormously rich and fiercely independent, divided her time between being an influential figure in court, and building and extending her properties, which included Chatsworth and Hardwick. She died in 1608, aged 90.

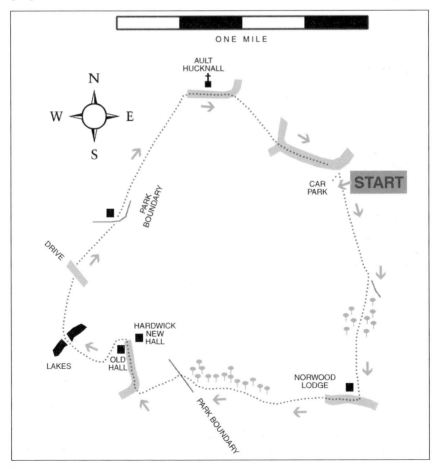

The Walk

This easy walk crosses pleasant arable fields before entering Hardwick Park and visiting both Hardwick Old and New Halls.

- Return to the white height barrier at the entrance to the car park. Pass through the barrier and immediately turn right over a stile by a metal field gate, signed 'Rowthorne Trail'.

- Follow the tree-lined, initially surfaced path for half-a-mile.

- After half-a-mile cross a stile onto a cross track. DO NOT go straight on over the stile ahead, with steps beyond, but turn right for 10 yards, to a stile into a field.

- Go half-left across the field towards woods.

- Cross a plank footbridge and enter the woods.

- Keep ahead up a clear path into trees. Follow this clear path, muddy in places, climbing steadily through the wood to a squeeze stile.

- Go through the stile and keep straight on across the field, aiming for houses seen ahead.

- Go through a squeeze stile in a wall, in front of a white house. Follow an enclosed gravelled footpath through the courtyard of Norwood Lodge to a stile leading onto a lane.

- Turn right along the tarmaced lane. Pass the entrance to Hardwick Park Farm on your right and keep straight on along the lane, now less well surfaced.

- At a gate across the lane, cross a stile to the right of the gate.

- Follow a footpath through a small wood, initially with an open field beyond the trees to the left. The path dips and climbs and soon runs along a band of trees, now with fields beyond the trees on both sides.

- Ignore a path to the left, but 20 yards later, in front of a field gate, turn left with the path and drop down the slope, with a wire fence on your left.

- In 80 yards you will reach a stile. Cross the stile and maintain your same line of advance along a clear path across open parkland, keeping a fence and trees up on your right.

- Follow the path to a kissing gate leading onto a drive.

- Turn right up the drive, passing an old pumping station on the right.

- Go through a kissing gate by a cattle grid and continue ahead up the drive. Soon you come to Hardwick Old Hall on your left, and Hardwick Hall on your right.

Hardwick Old Hall has grown organically over time. The original manor house of the de Hardwicke family stood on the site. In 1583 Bess, by then a rich lady, four times married and living at nearby Chatsworth, bought Hardwick Hall from her brother, who had inherited it. The following year she was forced to leave Chatsworth, which she had inherited from her second husband William Cavendish, under pressure from her fourth husband the Earl of Shrewsbury. She moved back into the family home at Hardwick and extended it piecemeal and hurriedly over the next five years. By 1588 the west wing had been added, including the Hill Great Chamber, a splendid third floor room with views from three sides, used for formal entertaining. An extra story was also put upon the original central block.

The following year an extra story was also added onto the east wing, into which was built the Forest Great Chamber, another formal dining/entertaining room, so-called because of the magnificent plaster wall decorations. These decorations, both here and in other rooms in Hardwick Old Hall, still survive and are one of the major attractions of the building.

Hardwick Old Hall took five years to convert from a simple manor house to a large and grandiose Hall, imperfect in design and inconvenient to use as a courtiers palace, but a useful trial run for the New Hall soon to be started.

Hardwick Old Hall is open April to November, Wednesday-Sunday 10am-6pm. Admission charge, free to members of English Heritage.

Work commenced on the new Hardwick Hall in 1590. Unlike the Old Hall, it was designed all as one piece, by Robert Smythson, who had also worked upon the Old Hall, and it was completed in 1597. It epitomises English Perpendicular domestic architecture, but with a grandeur and flamboyance rarely seen. It has massive tiers of windows, those in each floor larger than the one beneath, an ostentatious display of wealth at a time when glass was expensive. The interior is magnificent, with a high and light entrance hall leading to a Great Presence Chamber decorated with plaster bas relief by Abraham Smith. A Long Gallery, with twenty huge ceiling high windows, runs the length of the Hall. Inside the hall is an outstanding collection of furniture, tapestries and needlework dating from an inventory of 1601. The Hall is surrounded by a walled courtyard with gardens, orchards and an herb garden.

From the windows of her private chamber on the top floor Bess could look out for miles over the surrounding countryside, viewing her vast estates, and her other properties: Hardwick Old Hall next door: Sheffield Manor, one of her fourth husbands houses, to the north; also to the north Bolsover Castle (walk 15), home of her son Charles, and near to it the mansion of Oldcotes, which she built for another son, William; to the west are the hills which hide Chatsworth (walk 17), property of her second Husband, which see had also extended, and south of that another of her fourth husbands properties, Wingfield Manor (walk 12). Through marriage Bess had become one Derbyshire's major landowners, and certainly she became the greatest builder of her time in the county.

Why was Bess such a prodigious builder? One reason was for self-advertisement, advertising her wealth, taste and independence in a mans world. To ensure that her presence was felt, Hardwick Hall was topped with her initials twelve feet high, 'ES'

Hardwick New Hall.

or Elizabeth Salisbury. There is also a legend that she built in order to fulfil the prophesy of a family fortune teller, to the effect that she would not die whilst she was building. This is unlikely to be true, although there is a certain irony that Bess died in an unusually frosty February, when her builders were unable to work.

Open end March-end September, Wednesday, Thursday, Saturday and Sunday, 12.30pm-5.00pm. Admission charge, free to National Trust members.

● Stand with your back to the gates of Hardwick Hall.
Beside the gates is a fine example of a mounting block, used to enable gentlemen to climb onto their horses.

● Walk forward across the grass to a wall and fence. Turn left down the slope, with the high wall of the Old Hall grounds on your left and a fence on your right, to a kissing gate.

● Go through the kissing gate and turn sharp right down the slope aiming towards ponds seen in the dip ahead, keeping a wire fence on your right hand.

● At the bottom of the slope go through a kissing gate and across a causeway between two ponds.

Hardwick Park contains a fine herd longhorn cattle and also flocks of white-faced woodland sheep, which you will undoubtedly see during the next part of the walk.

● At the end of the short causeway go straight ahead across a cross-track, and go over a stile in the fence opposite. ✻

● Keep straight on up the edge of a field, keeping the fence on your right hand.

● In the top right-hand corner of the field, turn right through a pedestrian gate and then immediately turn left again, to continue the same line of advance, now with the fence on your left hand.

- Cross a drive. There is a cattle grid a few yards down the drive in front of you. DO NOT cross a stile by the cattle grid, but TURN RIGHT and walk uphill, keeping a fence on your left hand.
- At the top of the slope, bear half-left with the fence to a metal gate in front of houses.
- Go through the gate and keep straight on up the drive, with houses on your left and the park on your right.
- Follow the drive through a gate and across an open field, aiming for a church tower seen ahead.
- Follow the drive out onto a road at Ault Hucknall.
- Turn right along the road, passing the church and a farm on your left hand and a bungalow on your right.

Thomas Hobbes is buried in this church. Hobbes was a famous political philosopher best known for his book 'Leviathan', a treatise upon political theory defining the role of the state and still a classic today. He was employed for 60 years by William Cavendish and later by Bess of Hardwick as tutor to several generations of Cavendish children, and died aged 91 on a visit to Hardwick.

- Where the road bends sharp left, go through a metal field gate on the right.
- Take the right-most of two paths, and cross the field half-right from your former line of advance, aiming for a stile beside a conspicuous single tree.
- Cross this stile and go quarter-right across the next field, aiming for the corner of woods seen ahead.
- Cross over a stile into a lane. Turn right for 20 yards to a T-junction, where turn left, direction 'Rowthorne'.
- Follow the lane for quarter of a mile to reach the car park on your right.

* Instead, take RH stile - fence on LH

Dethick and the Babington Plot 1587

Distance: 5 miles

Map: OS sheet 119

Start and parking: The walk starts from the Village Hall in the centre of Holloway (grid ref: 325563), which faces the small green where Church Street joins Yew Tree Hill. Holloway is on a junction of minor roads just to the east of the A6, 3 miles south of Matlock. It is best approached either from Crich on the B3035, or from Cromford on the A6. There is ample street parking in Holloway.

Refreshments: Public House and shop in Holloway, shop in Lea.

Historical Background

Mary, the Catholic Queen of Scots, fled from her rebelling Protestant nobles in May 1568 and sought refuge in England. She expected either that her cousin Queen Elizabeth would help her to regain her throne, or that she would be allowed to go a sympathetic Catholic court on the continent. However, neither course of action was acceptable to Elizabeth. In the mid sixteenth century there was effectively a cold war raging, between on the one hand the powers of Catholic Europe, led by Spain, and on the other England, as the leader of the Protestant Northern Europe. Whilst Elizabeth deeply disapproved of a crowned monarch being deposed, she was happy for Scotland, always a troublesome neighbour, now to be Protestant controlled. She was also not prepared for Mary, who had a strong claim to the English throne, to be in the hands of her Catholic enemies, available for use as a pawn against Elizabeth. For the next 17 years Mary was confined in England under house arrest, for most of the time in or around Derbyshire, in various properties owned by the Earl of Salisbury (see walks 12, 13 and 17).

Mary's captivity did not remove her as a threat, for she was used as the passive focus of a number of plots against Elizabeth's life and throne, by English Catholics supported by Jesuit priests and Spanish money. Elizabeth's councillors constantly urged their queen to have Mary executed, but this Elizabeth absolutely refused without proof of Mary's active complicity in the plots. In 1586 that proof became available.

Mary in 1586 was held incommunicado at Chartley Manor, closely watched by the secret service of Sir Francis Walsingham. Walsingham arranged for supposedly secret coded letters to pass, hidden in beer barrels, between Mary and French Ambassador, letters actually deciphered and read by his agents before continuing their journey. One such letter came from a young Derbyshire gentleman, Anthony Babington, who had hatched a harebrained scheme to murder Elizabeth and place Mary on her throne, and asked Mary's advice upon

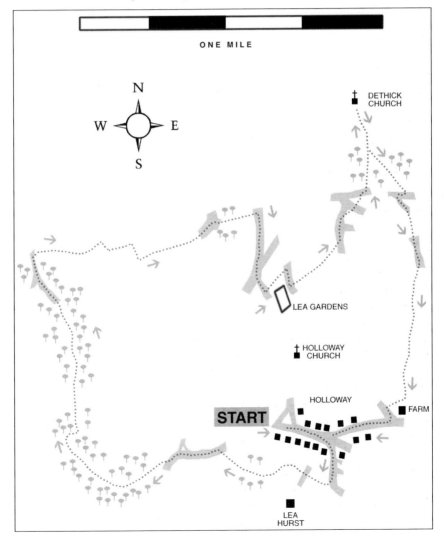

the plan. Mary, usually circumspect but now ill, dispirited and desperate, wrote back giving a tacit blessing to the conspiracy. Walsingham now had written evidence of Marys guilt in his hands. Mary was tried for treason, and executed at Elizabeth's order in February 1587.

The Walk

This walk goes through wooded hills and fields and visits the hamlet of Dethick, home of Anthony Babington. It also passes Lea Hurst, home to Florence Nightingale.

- With your back to the Village Hall, and facing the green, turn right and walk up Yew Tree Hill. Pass the Yew Tree public house and shortly after, turn right down Bracken Lane.

- Descend the hill, passing Thorpe Croft cul-de-sac and a second small close on your left.

- Where the road bends left, and just past a cottage on the right, turn right over a stile at a footpath sign.

- Go along an enclosed path for 60 yards, to reach a deer gate on your left. DO NOT turn left through the deer gate but go straight on through a swing gate into a field.

- Keep ahead along the bottom of the field, with a hedge on your left, to emerge onto the drive to Lea Hurst.

Florence Nightingale was born at the family home at Lea Hurst in 1820. The Nightingales were a very prosperous upper-class family, well- connected by marriage to a large circle of equally prosperous families, and apart from Lea Hurst they had another large country house in the New Forest and a town house in London's fashionable Mayfair. The young Florence and her sister divided their time between these properties, interspersed with visits to the Continent, all part of a fashionable social round of concerts, dances and dinner parties, whose sole objective for a woman of Florence's background was to find an eligible husband.

However, unlike her sister and her cousins, and all the other young ladies of her social circle, Florence was not content with this as a goal in life. She horrified her parents by expressing a desire to become a nurse, which in the middle of the nineteenth century was an occupation only engaged in by uneducated women from the lower classes.

Several eligible young men came to Lea Hurst to court Florence, but realising that marriage would not satisfy her needs, she rejected all comers. Instead, at the age of 30, she went to the family's New Forest home, where she took work as a volunteer nurse in Salisbury Hospital. At the outbreak of the Crimean War in 1854 she used her extensive family connections and influence to achieve a posting to the military hospital in Scutari. Here she was so appalled by the suffering and neglect she saw that she threw herself into overhauling the total system, in the teeth of complacent opposition from the army authorities. This opposition was battered into submission by her energy and personality, backed up by her social connections, which included the War Minister Sydney Herbert, a family friend.

In 1856 Florence returned to England a heroine at the end of the war. She came back to Lea Hurst and used it as a base from which to put the reforms she had started at Scutari to wider use. Florence was invited onto a Royal Commission set up to look at the Army Medical Department. By now she was a national figure, the darling of the public and the press, with the ear of Prince Albert. She used her popularity, her social connections and her wealth to merciless effect to force her ideas upon her fellow commissioners, even inviting Prime Minister Palmerston, a family friend, to Lea Hurst in order to canvass his support (see walk 24).

By 1861 reform of the Army Medical Service was compete and Florence turned her attentions to other issues, including hospital reform in general and the provision of formal training for nurses. To be near the centre of political power, she moved to the family home in London in 1862, and lived there until her death almost 50 years later, returning only rarely to Lea Hurst for increasingly fleeting visits.

- Cross the drive to go through a pedestrian gate. Keep straight on along the bottom of the next field, still with a hedge on your left.
- Enter the next field and keep ahead, keeping the wall of Lea Hurst close on your left hand. At the corner of the wall keep straight on to a stile.
- Cross the stile and follow the path through a stand of trees.
- Follow the path, now enclosed and with the deer park on your left, to a stile into an open field.
- Keep ahead down the field, with the wall on your right hand, to a kissing gate leading into a lane.
- Turn left down the lane into Lea Bridge.
- Pass the double end of a road to Lea and Riber on your right.

Up the road to the right is a mill built by John Smedley in 1784, one of the five hundred cotton mills, great and small, that sprang up in Derbyshire in the few decades that followed Arkwright's pioneering work at Cromford into the development of the factory system (see walk 20). Smedley was succeeded by his son, also John. This latter John was something of an eccentric who in the early 1850s decided to diversify into the newly emerging leisure industry in nearby Matlock. He built a hydropathic centre, a health farm designed to provide a full body service to wealthy guests, on the hilltop overlooking Matlock, constructing it as the mock-gothic folly, Riber Castle, which still dominates the town today.

- Cross over a bridge over the enclosed River Lea and pass David Bailey Motor Services to reach the road to Splash Farm. Do not turn up the road but go through a squeeze stile facing you, beside a wooden gate.

- Follow a path through woods, climbing through trees and bracken. The path curves to the right around the hillside, climbing steadily and with occasional views down into the valley below.
- The path levels off, passing under a tree growing in an arch over the path and meeting a wall on the right.
- 150 yards after the 'arch', and 80 yards after the end of the wall, turn right at a marker post onto a less distinct path, going uphill and back on yourself.
- The path meets a wall and turns sharp left in a zigzag up the hill.
- Follow the occasionally waymarked path as it zigzags up the hill, to meet a cross track at the top of the slope. There are signs on a tree to your right, for 'Cromford' and for 'the High Peak Trail'.
- Turn left along the cross track for 50 yards, to a stile into a field.
- Cross the stile and go half-right down the slope, to a clear path going through a gap between banks of bracken.

There are views across the valley to Holloway Church.

- Pass between the bracken banks, and swing left to a stile by a gate.
- Cross the stile and keep ahead along a clear path into woods, initially with a wall on the right.
- Follow the path as it undulates through woods to a gate.
- Cross the stile by the gate and keep straight on along a clear path up the slope ahead.
- The path climbs to a terrace and then continues steeply uphill. At the top of the second steep climb, turn right along a clear path through the trees, initially with the slope dropping away on your right hand.
- Climb the path for 100 yards to a stile by a wall.

There is a magnificent view ahead over Cromford, 'The birthplace of the Industrial Revolution', built as a model town to house his workers by Richard Arkwright (see walk 20).

- Cross the stile and immediately turn sharp right to follow a path through bracken, shortly meeting a wall on the right.
- Continue ahead, with the wall on your right hand, and the slope falling away to the left. Follow the path, overgrown in places, out to a cross track.
- Turn left along the cross track, with a wall on your right hand. In 30 yards a path joins from the left. Keep ahead up the track, now with a wall on the left and a bank and wall on the right.

There are occasional views down into Cromford and over Willersley Castle, built by Richard Arkwright as a 'palace' to be the crowning glory of his empire at Cromford. He died before it was completed.

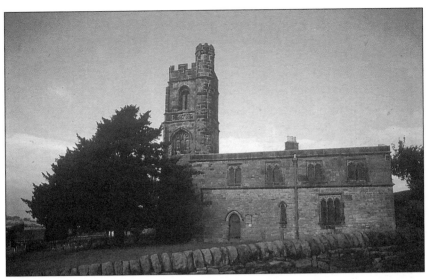

Dethick Church.

- In 200 yards, at a waymark sign, ignore a turning to the left but keep ahead along the walled track, following a blue-on-yellow marker.

- 75 yards later, turn right over a stile into a field, at a yellow on green marker.

- Keep ahead down the side of a field, with a hedge on your right hand, to a stile.

On the slope ahead, on the opposite side of the valley, is Dethick Church and surrounding hamlet, birthplace of Anthony Babington. Until the sixteenth century, Dethick was a typical example of a small agricultural settlement dominated by one family, in this case the Babingtons.

The family were disgraced after Anthony Babington's abortive plot to release Mary Queen of Scots, and they lost their lands and fortune. The hamlet we can see today consists of two farmhouses and a barn dating from the Babington era, together with the church, and remains little changed since the days when it was the personal property of the local landowner. Their manor house has long since been demolished.

- Cross the stile and keep ahead, still with a fence on your right hand. In 50 yards turn right with the field boundary, still with wall, fence and trees on your right, to a gate.

- DO NOT go through the gate but turn left and continue to follow the field boundary, still with wall, fence and trees on your right.

- Descend the field, passing through a line of trees to a gate.

- Go through the gate and follow a clear track to a stile beside the gate ahead.

- Go over the stile and go slightly left down the next field, on a waymarked path, aiming to keep Dethick, on the hillside opposite, straight ahead.

111

- Follow the path through a field boundary and descend the next field, maintaining the same line of advance, to meet a wall coming in from the left, at a gateway.

- Go through the gateway and up the waymarked track for 80 yards. Just before the track curves left, go right through a squeeze stile.

- Follow a path through a holly plantation, with a wall on your left hand.

- When there appear to be paths on your right, avoid dropping down the slope on the right, but follow the path up left to a squeeze stile.

- Go through the stile and turn right, down to stepping stones over a stream. Cross to a stile on the opposite bank.

- Keep ahead into a field. Go up the side of the field, with a wall on your right hand, to a stile into a lane.

- Turn right down the lane for 200 yards to a cross roads.

- Cross over and go up the road to Holloway and Crich, passing 30 mph signs.

- In 150 yards, just past a school sign, turn left at the drive of Old Chapel House. (There is a footpath sign on the opposite side of the road).

- Cross the entrance to the house's drive and go up steps into an enclosed footpath, with an ivy-covered wall on your right.

- Go through a squeeze stile and up the path through rhododendrons, out to a lane.

- Turn right up the lane, passing the entrance to Lea Gardens.

Lea Gardens are three acres of woodland garden, almost entirely given over to rhododendrons. It was laid down in Victorian times, when the fashion for rhododendrons was at its height, and this highly invasive plant was planted in huge numbers in country gardens throughout Britain.

The gardens are open to the public April to June daily. Entrance Fee.

- 100 yards past the entrance to the gardens, turn left through a kissing gate and follow an enclosed path for 300 yards to a lane.

- Turn left down the lane to join the end of a tarmaced road. Keep straight on down the road, passing between Lanes End on your left and Nightingale Cottage on your right.

- At a T-junction, keep straight on to a footpath across playing fields, to a kissing gate leading onto a road.

- Turn right up the road for 40 yards, then turn left down an enclosed footpath, signed 'Dethick and Tansley'.

- Follow the footpath down steps to a bridge, and up the other side to a stile into a field.

- Keep ahead along the field, with the wall on your left hand, to a stile.

● Cross the stile and keep straight on up the next field to Dethick Church.

Until the sixteenth century, the hamlet of Dethick was the personal property of the Babington family. The Babingtons were yeoman farmers who had owned the rights to the surrounding lands since Norman times, and had grown in wealth and status to become important gentry in the area. They had built a sturdy manor house, attached to their farm, and surrounded by the houses of their farm workers and retainers. Nothing now remains of the manor house, but the farm buildings remain.

The Norman church of St John the Baptist at Dethick was largely maintained by grants from the Babington family, who lived in a manor house just behind the church and whose farm and retainers homes comprised the hamlet of Dethick. The church was in the Babington's 'gift' – they appointed and paid the salary of a vicar, who would have also lived within the hamlet. The Babingtons were Catholics, and it is likely that they employed the occasional secret services of a Catholic priest in the privacy of their house, whilst continuing their social duty of paying for the upkeep of a Protestant priest in their church.

Roman Catholicism had been banned in England since Henry VIII had broken with Rome in 1534 and made protestantism the state religion. Many of his subjects remained Catholic at heart however, and a sizeable minority continued to practice the Catholic religion. Elizabeth had made considerable attempts to undo the strife caused by the religious fervour of her two predecessors, Edward VI and Mary, and her reign showed a remarkable degree of religious tolerance. Despite the fact that the leading Catholic powers of Europe were attempting to undermine her throne, Elizabeth turned a blind eye to her Catholic subjects. They were allowed to secretly practice their religion, provided they remained loyal to her. In return, although a fanatical minority of English Catholics favoured Elizabeth's murder and replacement with her Catholic cousin Mary, as urged by the Pope, most were loyal to their queen and content with the present regime.

Anthony Babington had taken the road to social advancement usual in his day, and entered service as a page to his local lord the Earl of Salisbury, husband of the formidable Bess of Hardwick (see walk 13). Salisbury was the owner of many fine properties in Derbyshire, and the gaoler to Mary Queen of Scots. Babington met Mary whilst she was staying at Wingfield Manor five miles to the south (see walk 12) and according to legend, frequently visited her disguised as a gypsy. Babington, hopelessly romantic and fanciful, conceived a wild plan wherein he and six companions would assassinate Elizabeth, meet a Catholic army that would land in England (which existed only in his imagination) and lead it to Derbyshire to rescue a grateful Mary. No real measures were taken to keep his impractical plans secret, which led to the downfall of Mary. Babington was arrested, tried and executed as a traitor, and his family disgraced.

The church here at Dethick contains the tombs of several members of the Babington Family, although not Anthony, whose remains were buried in an unmarked grave near Lincoln's Inn Fields in London.

The church is kept locked for security, but the key can be obtained from the nearby farm if you wish to visit it.

- After you have seen the church, leave the churchyard the way you entered, and retrace your steps across the first field to the stile.

- Cross the stile and now bear half-left across the field, veering away from the wall on your right, to a stile into the woods ahead.

- Cross the stile and follow a path down through trees to a narrow footbridge.

- Cross the bridge and turn left up a railed path to a road.

- Turn right along the road for 100 yards. Just past Lea Chapel on your left, turn sharp left up a track, signed 'Upper Holloway and Wakebridge'.

- Follow the track to its end. Cross a stile and go half-right across a field to a stile.

- Go through two squeeze stiles into a field. Maintain the same line of advance, cutting across the corner of the field to a stile leading down into a sunken track.

- Turn right up the sunken track. Ignore a side turn in 30 yards but keep straight on.

- The path emerges at the end of a farmtrack by a yellow metal gate. Keep straight on along the track for 100 yards, to where the track turns right. Do not turn with the track but cross a stile in front of you.

- Keep ahead across the field, generally following the right-hand boundary, to a footpath post by a metal gate.

- Cross the stile and go quarter-left across the field, passing just to the left of a single tree 50 yards ahead, and maintaining your line of advance across the brow of the hill to a footpath sign by a gate ahead.

To the left can be seen the monument to the Sherwood Foresters, The Nottinghamshire & Derbyshire Regiment, standing on top of Crich Stand. It was erected in 1923 on Crich Cliff, 950 feet above sea level, to commemorate the men of the regiment who died in World War One. Three successive beacon towers had stood on this spot in the past: all had been destroyed by lightning. There is still a beacon light on the present tower, which is turned on at dusk and visible for miles.

- Go through the gate and down the left-hand edge of the field towards the farm ahead. Pass to the right of the farm, aiming for a stile in the wall 50 yards to the right of the barn.

- Cross the stile and turn left down the lane, passing the farm to reach 'Upper Holloway'.

- Turn right down Upper Holloway for quarter of a mile to reach the main road.

- Bracken Road is just opposite to the left. Turn right back to the Village Hall.

Walk 15

Bolsover Castle and the early Stuarts

Distance: 5.5 miles

Map: OS sheet 120

Start and parking: Free car park opposite the entrance to Bolsover castle (grid ref: 472705) Bolsover is on the A632, three miles north of junction 29 of the M1. The castle is just south of the main street, and is clearly signposted from both approach roads into town.

Refreshments: Public houses, shops and café in Bolsover.

Historical Background

Inigo Jones, the father of English architecture, enjoyed the patronage of James I. He introduced into England a new style of building known as the 'Palladian', that was very formalised and based upon the architecture of classical Greece and Rome. James's son Charles I had a great interest in the visual arts and in architecture, and his accession to the throne in 1625 brought a new vigour to these areas. Charles was also a knowledgeable connoisseur of paintings. Under his patronage artists such as Rubens and Van Dyke were encouraged to settle in England and form the nucleus of a new and vibrant school of art, very romantic and influenced by images from the classics. There was an explosion of building, public and private, conforming to Jones' fashion and incorporating the new ideas in painting and sculpture in abundance.

Sir William Cavendish, Earl of Newcastle, was one of many courtiers who rose to prominence in the Stuart court, and he rebuilt the family home at Bolsover as the epitome of the building and interior design of the age. He was also an accomplished horseman, in the Haute Ecole school of riding, which requires horses to be put through complex, almost balletic movements, and built an indoor riding school into the castle. Charles was so intrigued by reports of the transformation of Bolsover that he and his queen Henrietta Maria visited the castle in 1634: in their honour Cavendish put on a masque, a lavish entertainment written by Ben Johnson and designed by Inigo Jones, costing £15,000 (the equivalent of £1,000,000 today).

Cavendish was a loyal supporter of the King. He used his fortune to help fund Charles at the start of the Civil War in 1642. He ably led the Royalist forces in the North of England in the first years of the war and fought at Marston Moor in 1644, the battle that ended Charles' hopes of a military victory. After Marston Moor, Cavendish decided the royalist cause was lost and went into exile in Holland, where he remained until the restoration in 1660. He was rewarded by Charles II by being created 1st Duke of Newcastle. Whilst in exile he wrote a textbook on riding, *A general system of horsemanship*, which was to be a classic for the next two centuries.

The civil war and his subsequent exile had bankrupted Cavendish, but upon his return he determined to make the war-damaged Bolsover Castle habitable again. He spent the next 15 years, until his death in 1676 restoring the castle, which today remains one of the greatest examples of Jacobean Romantic architecture in the country.

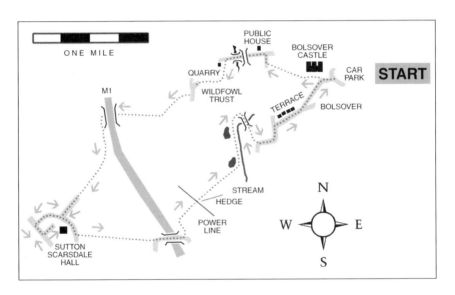

The Walk

This walk crosses little walked countryside to the ruins of Sutton Scarsdale Hall, before returning through Carr Vale Nature reserve to Bolsover Castle.

A history of Bolsover Castle is given at the end of the walk.

- With your back to the castle entrance drive, turn right along the road (Castle Street), passing an infants school on your right.

- In 50 yards, where Castle Street turns left, keep straight on down the railed pavement along Castle Lane.

- Descend steeply, bearing right with the road.

There are extensive views to the left, looking over the Vale of Scarsdale. In the seventeenth century almost all the land you can see was owned by the Earls of Newcastle. There was an extensive deer park in the valley, used for hunting by the Earl and his guests; there was a manor farm, worked exclusively on the Earls behalf; and there were a number of other farms and smallholding, worked by tenants who paid an annual rent to the Earl. There was also an embryonic coal-mining industry. Coal was becoming important and was mined on the Earl's land, mainly by open-cast methods but also with some shallow-pit excavation. The site of those early seventieth century mines was on the far side of the more extensive but now closed workings seen in the valley in front of you.

Sutton Scarsdale Hall, the turning point of this walk, can be seen on the ridge directly in front of you, beyond the motorway.

- Where the road bears left 60 yards later, keep straight on up a tree and hedge-lined footpath.
- Follow the footpath, with a fence on your left hand.
- Just after the fence on the left ends, at a fork in the path, take the left fork down to the top of a field.
- On entering the field, go half-right down the slope, aiming for the chimneys of the works seen ahead, and the middle of a row of white houses on the road below. You soon pick up a path across the field.
- Go through a gap in the bottom hedge, 10 yards to the left of the bottom right-hand corner of the field. Keep straight ahead across the next field, aiming just to the right of a row of houses seen ahead.
- Join the hedge around the last house, and walk with the hedge on your left hand, out to a lane.
- Turn right along the lane to the main road, opposite The Castle Arms public house.
- Turn left along the road (you may prefer to cross to the opposite side, where there is a pavement) and walk with the road on your left hand side.
- Go down the road for 600 yards, passing the entrance to Bolsover Business Park, then over one railway bridge and under one (disused) one.
- 50 yards past the bridge, cross a river and pass 'derestricted' signs, and 10 yards later turn left over a stile at a waymark sign, into the corner of a paddock.
- Turn left along the paddock, keeping the fence and hedge on your left.
- At the far end, leave the paddock through a gap in the fence on your left.
- With your back to the gap, go ahead for 10 yards to reach a cross track.
- Turn right along the track. In 50 yards cross a quarry road and keep ahead to a metal gate across a broad green track.

- Go up the track, with a wire fence on your right and reeds and trees off to the left.

- Continue along the track for 150 yards, with a disused quarry and two ponds on your right.

- Swing right with the track around the end of the second pond.

- Climb the bank with the track and keep ahead along a grassy embankment between disused quarries.

- At the end of the embankment, keep straight on and descend onto a quarry road.

- Turn left down the quarry road to a T-junction at the bottom of the slope. Here turn left and go along the quarry road through gate posts.

- Follow the road for 100 yards, until you reach a 'Derbyshire Wildfowl Trust' board on your left, just as a lake comes into view on the left.

- Turn right opposite the board. Leave the road and go through a gap in the fence into the bottom right-hand corner of a large field. *NB. Although this is a public footpath, there is no sign nor stile at this point to denote its existence.*

- Go half-left, crossing the field on a diagonal and aiming 100 yards to the right of a single tree standing half-way along the opposite side.

- 100 yards to the right of the tree, at an angle in the adjoining field boundary, is a stile beside a metal field gate. Cross the stile and turn right up the field, with the hedge on your right hand.

Bolsover Castle.

- At the top of the field go through a gate and keep ahead, now along a track, still with the hedge on your right.
- At the bottom of the next field, keep ahead and follow the track through an arch under the motorway.
- Immediately through the arch cross a stile by a gate and turn left. Walk along the field, with the motorway embankment on your left.
- Cross a stile into the next field and keep straight on.
- At the end of the field cross a stile and keep straight on along an enclosed track.
- Leave the track and bear right, keeping the fence on your right hand and leaving the motorway. Go down the side of the field.
- 80 yards down the side of the field, turn right over a stile.
- Go half-left across the next large field, aiming for the left-most of three trees standing on the opposite side, more or less in line with Sutton Scarsdale Hall on the hill behind.
- Join a track just to the right of the tree. Keep ahead up the concrete track across the field, with the Hall to your left front. *NB the actual right of way is some yards to the right of this track but seems to be invariably ploughed up.*
- Follow the track to the ditch and wall in front of Sutton Scarsdale Hall.

This ditch and wall are what is technically known as a 'Ha-Ha'. These were popular in the eighteenth and nineteenth centuries, and were built around the grounds of a house to keep cattle from staying onto the lawns and gardens, but at the same time avoiding obstructing the view from the house windows with a wall.

- To visit the Hall, turn right with the track, keeping the Ha-Ha on your left. Follow the track as it swings left through the farmyard and out to a road.
- Turn left along the road for 80 yards, then turn left down a side road, signed to 'Sutton Scarsdale Hall'.

Sutton Scarsdale Hall was built between 1724 and 1729 for Nicholas Leake, the 4th and last Earl of Scarsdale, on the site of earlier buildings dating from 1489. The architect Francis Smith of Warwick was employed to build this stately mansion. The Scarsdale family had been lords of the manor of Sutton Scarsdale since 1485, when Henry VII granted land to them that had previously been held by supporters of the deposed Richard III. The 4th Earl, sometime ambassador to the Holy Roman Empire and the model for Hogarth's 'Rakes Progress', built this huge and ostentatious Hall to prove his importance in the neighbourhood and to impress visitors from London. The costs of building the Hall were prohibitive, and the Earl died in debt in 1736.

The Hall was eventually bought in 1820 by the son of Richard Arkwright, the famous industrialist (see walk 20) who was heir to his fathers commercial empire and wanted to demonstrate that he was now part of the landed gentry. It remained in the Arkwright family until 1919, when the last member of the family, William Arkwright died childless. (William was left crippled and impotent after a riding accident and became the model for the husband in DH Lawrence's Lady Chatterley's Lover.*) The house was eventually bought by a speculator who sold some of the fittings, including the whole Venetian Drawing room, to american museums. Since then the Hall has been allowed to fall into quiet ruin.*

Open April-November, 10am-6pm. Admission free.

⬤ After visiting the Hall, return through the farmyard the way you came, and then continue ahead along the track along the bottom of the Halls lawn, keeping the Ha-Ha on your right.

⬤ Where the Ha-Ha curves sharp right, turn left and follow the track down towards a farm in the dip below.

The strategic position of Bolsover Castle, on a ridge that dominates the Vale of Scarsdale, can clearly be seen. The original castle, of which nothing now remains, was built by William Peveril who had built the castle at Castleton (see walk 9). William, the bastard son of William the Conqueror, was given extensive lands in Derbyshire, to hold on behalf of his father. In common with standard Norman practice, castles were built, partly for strategic reasons, but also to overawe the local conquered population with the power of Norman might. Bolsover commands a north-south route along the valley, but the psychological impact of its position is immediately apparent.

⬤ Follow the track out to a lane and turn left.

⬤ Follow the lane downhill and right, to pass over the motorway.

⬤ Immediately over the motorway, turn left over a stile and up a track, with the motorway on your left.

⬤ At the point where the track curves right away from the motorway and towards a ruined farm, leave the track and go half-right across an open field. *NB there is no footpath sign or waymark to indicate the path at this point, although it is visible on the ground.*

⬤ Pass under powerlines on the far side of the field, at a point where a hedge comes up to join the lines at a right angle, making a boundary between two fields.

⬤ Standing facing the hedge, the right of way goes a third-right across the left-most of the two fields. If the path is not apparent on the ground, aim at the spire of a church seen on the horizon, some way to the right of the castle.

⬤ Cross a stile at the bottom of the field. Go half-left across the meadow beyond, curving around the pond, to a stile in the trees in the far left-hand corner of the field.

⬤ Cross the stile and the gully beyond to another stile. Cross this and keep ahead, with the stream on your right hand.

- Follow the path as it curves right, at a Carr Vale Nature Reserve sign.
- Follow the path past an angling lake on your left to steps. Go up the steps and turn right across a footbridge.
- Keep ahead along the tarmaced path, following it as it swings left to a kissing gate going onto a track.
- Turn left along the track. At the end of the field on your left, at a junction, turn left with the track. Pass garages on your right hand side to reach the corner of a terrace of houses.
- Turn right up the street, with the terrace on your left and allotments and soon a playing field on your right.
- Cross over Chapel Road and continue up the road, passing a primary school and then allotments on your left.
- After the end of the allotments, turn left up Castle Lane, and follow this steeply uphill.
- At the top of Castle Lane, keep straight on for the Castle and the car park.

The first Bolsover Castle was built by William Peveril, but forfeited to the crown when his son fell from favour for assassinating the Earl of Derby. During the Barons Revolt against King John, the Earl of Derby captured and held the castle on behalf of the king. The castle then passed through numerous hands until being granted to Sir George Talbot, 5th Earl of Shrewsbury in 1533, by which time it had ceased to have any strategic value.

The second George Talbot, the 6th Earl, married Bess of Hardwick in 1568 (see walk 13) and the two families were further united with the marriage of their eldest two sons and daughters. The 6th Earl largely bankrupted himself doing his duty as custodian of Mary Queen of Scots for 16 years (see walk 14), and to restore some of the family fortune his son Gilbert, the 7th Earl, first rented and then ultimately sold Bolsover to his brother-in-law and step-brother Sir Charles Cavendish, Bess's youngest son.

Cavendish chose Robert Smythson, who had already designed Hardwick Hall for his mother (see walk 13) to design a new castle at Bolsover. The building of the 'Little Castle', the square mock-fortress, commenced in 1614 in the style of the Tower of London's White Tower, on the ruins of the old Norman keep. When Sir Charles and Smythson both died, Cavendish's son William employed Smythson's son John to carry on the work. By then Inigo Jones was setting new standards of fashion and design, and the Little Castle was embellished with balconies and panelling, and its rooms painted with extravagant classical allegories, in the style known as Jacobean Romantic.

The Little Castle was finished in 1621 and work commenced on the rest of the castle. By then William was an important man in the court of the new king Charles I, and he added a new range of buildings, with sufficient apartments and kitchens to cater for his increased number of guests and visitors. He also added the Riding School Range, which with forge, harness room, indoor exercise paddock and viewing gallery allowed him to indulge in his hobby to the full.

Cavendish led the Royalist armies in northern England in the early years of the Civil War, using Bolsover Castle as his base. He fled the country following the defeat of the royalists at the battle of Marston Moor in 1644, an act viewed as desertion by many of his comrades-in-arms. The castle surrendered to Parliamentarian forces and the defensive outer walls and strong doors were demolished. The castle was also stripped of all materials of any value. Upon his return from exile, Cavendish set about restoring the castle. The work was carried on by his successors, and today Bolsover stands as the finest example of early Stuart architecture and interior design in England.

Open April-November, 10am-6pm daily; November to March, Wednesday-Sunday, 10am-4pm. Admission charge, free to members of English Heritage.

Walk 16

Eyam and the Great Plague 1665-6

Distance: 4.5 miles

Map: OS sheet 119

Start and parking: The walk starts from the pay & display car park in the middle of Eyam (grid ref: 215768) Eyam is on the B6521, half a mile north of the A623 Chesterfield to Stockport road, 14 miles west of Chesterfield.

Refreshments: Shops, tearooms, and public houses in Eyam and in Stoney Middleton.

Historical Background

Throughout the Middle Ages plague had been the scourge of Britain. The population, especially in the towns, lived in very close proximity to each other, sanitation was virtually non-existent, and personal hygiene minimal. Although it came in several forms, 'plague' was a specific disease, carried by the rat flea. When circumstances were right the plague virus would multiply rapidly, decimating their rodent hosts and then spreading to the human population.

The plague had visited Britain many times, most devastatingly in 1348 when, known as the Black Death, bubonic plague slaughtered a third of the population. The plague of 1665-6, later known as the Great Plague, was probably pneumonic plague. It appeared in London at Christmas 1664, but an unusually cold winter kept it bay until the following Easter. With the arrival of warmer weather the plague spread with frightening rapidity through the narrow, unsanitary streets of London. Those who could afford to flee the city did so, by and large the richer inhabitants: those who could not, stayed and died in their thousands. By February 1666, when the plague had finally run its course, nearly 100,000 out of a population of half a million were dead.

The plague was not confined to London. It was highly infectious and easy to transmit, and was often carried by the very people who were fleeing it. In September 1665 it reached the tiny Derbyshire village of Eyam, brought by a travelling tailor. By the end of October, 30 out of a population of 350 were already dead. Some of the surviving population started to leave the village in panic. The rector, the Revd. William Mompesson, realised that this would only serve to spread the plague. Supported by his predecessor Thomas Stanley, he called a meeting of the full community and argued strongly and emotionally that the villagers should stay in Eyam and let the plague run its course rather than spreading it throughout the county. With an amazing heroism the villagers agreed to this course of action. Their decision was communicated to neighbouring villages, who left food and supplies at designated spots, and Eyam was left to its self-imposed quarantine. By the time the plague finally disappeared, 267 out of 350 villagers had died.

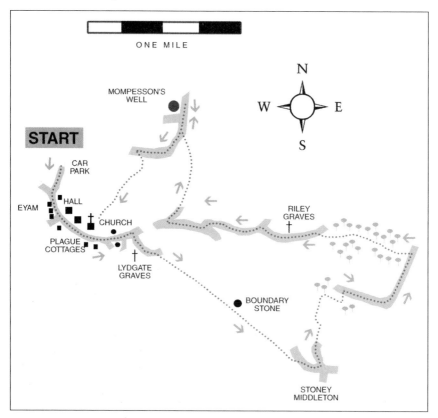

The Walk

This walk goes around the village of Eyam, following the historic course of the plague of 1665-6, then crosses the open moor to Stoney Middleton and returns though wooded hills to Eyam.

● From the car park turn left and return to the main street through Eyam, noting the water trough on the right on your way down the hill.

Many cities, towns and villages in Britain did not have supplies of clean drinking water until the mid- nineteenth century. Eyam was unusual in having a public water supply from 1588 onwards. The village stands on a spring line, where the shale of the valley meets the millstone grit above. Rainwater seeps into the porous millstone grit and surfaces at the less porous shales as springs. At least ten sets of drinking troughs, of which this is one, collected spring water and distributed it for drinking, washing and agricultural use throughout the village.

● Turn left along the main street, soon reaching Eyam Hall on your left and the village green on your right.

Eyam Hall was built in 1671 by Thomas Wight for his son John, to impress the latters bride-to-be, a rich local heiress named Elizabeth Kniveton. It is an excellent example of a seventeenth-century yeoman's house, built of local millstone grit. A western, kitchen, wing built from limestone was added in 1700, since when the house has been very little altered. The initials of its first occupant, E and J, can be seen on the lead down pipes.

Eyam Hall is open April to November, Wednesday, Thursday and Sunday 11.00am-4.30pm. Admission charge.

The tiny village green has the old market hall behind it, where local farmers would bring their produce into town for sale. The stocks on the green were first installed in the late eighteenth century, to discipline unruly lead miners who would come into town on a friday night and celebrate the weekend too disruptively.

● 100 yards past the Hall are the 'plague cottages' on your left, with marker boards.

The plague started in these three cottages. George Viccars, a travelling tailor, lodged in the centre cottage with the widowed Mrs Cooper and her two sons. Cloth, sent to Viccars from plague-ridden London, was damp on arrival and placed before an open fire to dry. Viccars inhaled the plague bacillus thus released, and died a few days later, on 7 September 1665. At the time no one recognised the symptoms he displayed – a rosy, ringlike rash and pronounced sneezing, followed shortly by collapse and death. (These symptoms were soon commemorated in the innocent sounding nursery rhyme 'Ring-a-ring a roses, a pocketful of posies, atishoo, atishoo, we all fall down.')

Two weeks later one of the sons, Edward Cooper, died, followed the next day by Peter Halksworth, who lived next door. Four days later Thomas Thorpe, who lived in the cottage the other side, died, shortly followed by his wife and by the second Cooper son, Jonathan. The plague had arrived.

● Continue along the road, passing the church.

The church of St Lawrence is twelfth century, although its foundations are Saxon and its history as a religious centre even older. After the Romans withdrew from Britain, the Christian religion they had introduced was driven underground as waves of pagan invaders swept in from Scandinavia, Germany and the Low Countries. When Christian missionaries started to re-establish Christian worship in northern England from the seventh century onwards, they found no formal churches left, and so had to preach on the open moors. To mark where such services would take place, preaching crosses were erected at strategic points on the moors to mark where congregations should gather to listen to itinerant preachers. There is a magnificent preaching cross in the churchyard of St Lawrence's dating from the eighth century. It is Celtic in design, betraying the origins of the early missionaries, and it is now truncated: the top cross rests upon a column that has lost five or six feet of its origin height. The cross would originally have been painted to highlight the religious images.

The Revd. William Mompesson was rector of St Lawrence's. His predecessor, Thomas Stanley, still lived in Eyam, but had left the church because he was unable to take the oath under the Act of Uniformity, binding all public figures to a strict form of Anglicanism. It was to this church that the two men called the villagers of Eyam in October 1665 and implored them not to leave the village and thus spread the plague.

- Continue along the road as it curves left and descends. Ignore a turn to the right but keep ahead to the Bull Ring at the village centre.

The Bull Ring was the old centre of the village. As is name implies, it is where, upon public holidays, a live bull would be tethered and torn apart by mastiffs, for the entertainment of the crowd. This barbaric 'sport' was not finally banned until 1835.

- Cross over the bull ring to a pillar box and telephone kiosk, just before the Eyam Tea Rooms, and take the narrow lane leading off to the right, Lydgate.
- Climb the hill with the lane, passing Rose & Fossil Cottage, and soon passing a walled enclosure on your right.

The walled enclosure surrounds the Lydgate Graves, where plague victims George Darby and his daughter Mary are buried. Mary died in September 1666, one of the last victims of the plague which had swept the village for the previous 12 months. By the time she died, only eighty of the 350 villagers who had attended Mompesson's meeting and agreed to quarantine themselves for the duration of the plague were still alive. (On the walls of many of the old cottages in Eyam there are numerous plaques, commemorating those who died, and marking with the dates of death the spread of the plague through the community. Walking around the village reading the plaques is a rewarding but sobering experience.)

- Continue along the lane for 100 yards past the Lydgate graves. At a small green triangle, DO NOT go down left with the lane but keep straight on, along a footpath signed 'Stoney Middleton'.
- Follow the track past cottages and through three gates to enter open fields.
- Continue along the track through two fields.
- At the end of the second field, do not go through the gate, but go through a squeeze stile on the left and continue ahead along an enclosed footpath.
- At the end of the footpath keep ahead on a distinct path across open moor, with the cliff away to your right hand.

● Just before passing a stand of trees on your left, you come to the boundary stone. *The large boulder with several weathered holes in the top, is the Boundary Stone. At the time of the plague Eyam, like most rural communities, was largely self sufficient, but there were still some provisions that needed to be brought in from outside. The villagers arranged that the inhabitants of neighbouring villages should come no closer to Eyam than this remote boulder. Provisions were to be left here, and coins left in payment on top of the stone, in the holes which were to be filled with vinegar as a primitive but effective disinfectant.*

● Pass the stand of trees and continue ahead down the slope, aiming for the white houses seen in the valley below.

● At the bottom of the slope cross a stile into a lane and turn right.

● Follow the lane to pass a chapel on your left. Immediately past a telephone box, turn left up 'The Fold'.

Stoney Middleton with its shops and refreshments is down to your right.

● Follow the lane, which soon becomes unsurfaced, past houses to a step stile beside two gates.

● Cross the stile and go along the side of the field, keeping the wall immediately on your left hand. Ignore two field gates but follow the wall around a corner, into the very top left-hand corner of the field, to go through a gate beside a footpath sign.

● Go up the side of the field, with the wall on your right hand, ignoring a pedestrian gate in 10 yards, to go to the top of the field and through a field gate.

● Go half-left across the corner of a field to a squeeze stile.

● Go through the stile and turn right up the field, keeping the wall on your right hand, to a squeeze stile in the top corner.

● Go through the stile and turn right along a footpath, a fence on your left and trees on your right. Follow the footpath, somewhat overgrown at times, along the edge of the woods.

● Near the top of the slope, look out for a sharp left hand turn. (Opposite the turn there is a waymark on the wall on your right, pointing downhill.) Turn left and climb steeply up thorough trees.

● Soon a wall is joined. Keep left along the wall, with the wall on your right hand, to a stile and steps leading up onto a road.

● Turn right along the road for half a mile, following it around a left hand bend, 350 yards past the bend, turn left up a narrow track, actually an unmarked footpath, climbing between field boundaries.

● Follow the path for quarter of a mile, climbing steadily through trees, with views down to the left eventually emerging.

- Continue along the footpath, now level and with a steep slope on your left, to join a track.

- Turn left along the track for 200 yards, to reach the Riley Graves in walled enclosure in the field to the right.

These graves are one of the most poignant memorials to the plague and its effect. The Hancock family lived here, in an isolated cottage. With their own small-holding, their own hens and their own well, they tried to remain self-contained and avoid contact with the village as far as possible. It was to no avail: of the eight members of the family, seven died within a week of each other, in August 1666, to be buried here by the mother, the sole survivor.

- Continue along the lane, soon to join a tarmaced lane. Turn left down this.

- The land joins a road on the edge of Eyam. Turn right along the road for 300 yards, then turn right up 'Riley Back Lane'.

- Follow the tarmaced lane uphill past houses. Where the lane ends, keep straight on up a track.

- Follow the wall on your left for 100 yards, then fork right up a broad track into woods. Ignore all side turns and climb steadily.

- At the top of the slope, join a wall and keep ahead, the wall on your right hand. Follow the path, soon with a steep sided stream on your left, to reach a road.

- Turn right along the road for 200 yards, ignoring a side turn to Bretton, to reach Mompesson's Well.

Like the boundary stone on the other side of the village, this well was another spot where provisions would be left by neighbours, in return for coins disinfected in a pool of vinegar at the lip of the well. After the event, the well was renamed in commemoration of the rector whose foresight had stopped the plague from being spread.

- Leave the well and retrace your steps back down the road for quarter of a mile, passing the footpath you came up and going around a long right-hand bend.

- Go through a pedestrian gate on the left, marked 'Eyam via Churchyard' and descend the field, with the wall on your right hand.

- Cross the wall in the bottom corner of the field and continue down the next field, with the wall now on your left.

- In the bottom left-hand corner of the field, go through a stile to the right of a gate and keep ahead sown an enclosed footpath.

- At the end of the footpath go through the gate into the churchyard, and keep ahead to reach the road.

Several victims of the plague are buried in the churchyard, although such was the

The Riley Graves, Eyam.

volume of bodies that most were buried near where they died. Catherine Mompesson was the wife of the rector and his staunch supporter, not only at the beginning, when he set about persuading his flock not to flee, but also during the long dark months that followed, when Mompesson must have questioned the cost his arguments were exacting. Catherine died in August 1666, 220th victim of the plague, and her tomb can be seen in the graveyard, beside the old Saxon cross. There is also a memorial to Thomas Stanley, who survived the plague and was later buried here in the graveyard, although not under his present plaque.

⬤ Turn right along the road back to the car park.

Chatsworth House and the Glorious Revolution 1688

Distance: 6.5 miles

Map: OS sheet 119

Start and parking: This walk starts from Calton Lees free car park (grid ref: 257686). The car park on the west side of the B6012, which runs from Baslow to Matlock, through Chatsworth Park.

Refreshments: Shop and seasonal tearoom in Edensor. Occasional tearoom in Chatsworth garden centre.

Historical Background

In 1688 England faced a major crisis. The Civil War forty years previously had resulted in the ascendancy of Parliament and the Protestant religion. Upon the restoration of the monarchy the pragmatic Charles II had not tried, overtly at least, to undermine this settlement. His brother and successor James II, however, tried his best to pull power back from Parliament and to re-establish the Catholic faith. James was initially tolerated although his views upon government were intensely disliked. He was after all 52 when he came to the throne in 1685 and had two Protestant and more liberal daughters to succeed him. However in 1688 he produced a male heir, who would be brought up a Catholic and would take precedence over his sisters. Leading parliamentarians decided that James was too dangerous to be left on the throne, and plotted his removal.

The plotters had a horror of disrupting the social order they headed by unlocking the doors to civil war again. They also knew that a purely internal uprising would not succeed, since James had greatly strengthened the standing army and distributed it to key points in the country. So seven of England's most influential men signed an invitation to William, Prince of Orange, leader of the Protestant cause in Europe and husband of James' eldest daughter Mary, to invade England and restore his wife as 'legitimate' heir to the throne. One of the seven was William Cavendish, 4th Earl of Devonshire, owner of estates at Chatsworth.

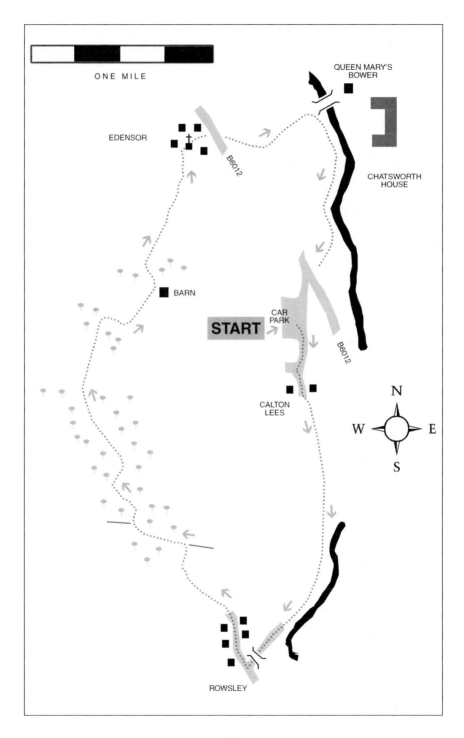

ONE MILE

QUEEN MARY'S BOWER

EDENSOR

B6012

CHATSWORTH HOUSE

BARN

START

CAR PARK

B6012

CALTON LEES

N

W   E

S

ROWSLEY

On 5 November 1688 William of Orange landed at Torbay at the head of an army, and the plotters rose in his favour. Cavendish, at the head of a force of loyal retainers, marched from Derbyshire and seized Nottingham, thus dominating the north-south routes of England. There were simultaneous risings in Yorkshire and Chester. James' second daughter, Anne, fled from London to Nottingham and put herself under Cavendish's protection. Encouraged by the popular risings, James' army started to desert him, and on Christmas Day James fled to France. Parliamentary rule and the Protestant faith were secured by the accession of Mary and her husband William.

Cavendish was rewarded for his part in 'The Glorious Revolution' with a Dukedom. As part of the clique around the new King, he soon became one of the most influential men in England, and decided to rebuild his country home at Chatsworth as a palace befitting his position.

The Walk

This walk goes across the wooded and hilly countryside around Rowsley before returning though the rolling Chatsworth Park to visit Chatsworth House, finally following the banks of the Derwent back to the start.

- Stand in the Calton Lees car park, facing the B6012 and with the hill behind you. Turn right along the tarmaced minor road at the foot of the car park, initially parallel to the B6012.

- Pass the trades entrance to Chatsworth Garden Centre and toilets on your left and keep straight on down the road, through gates marked 'No through road'.

- Continue down the road for 600 yards to a cross track. DO NOT continue ahead up the track through a gate, but turn sharp left with the tarmaced road. Pass Calton Lees Farm on your right and Calton Lees House on your left.

- At the end of the last cottage, where the road ends, keep straight ahead to cross a step stile in the wall ahead.

- Immediately over the stile turn left and follow the path around the bottom of the field, keeping a wall on your left hand.

- At the far end of the field, cross the wall by a ladder stile and maintain the same direction along a track, now with the wall on your right.

- Follow the track through a gate and continue straight on across the middle of the next field, aiming for a gate in the wall on the far side, directly ahead.

- Pass though the gate and continue quarter-left through the middle of the next field. It will initially appear that you are aiming for the woodland ahead.

- Follow the field as it curves left and narrows, now with the river away to your left.

- Near the bottom corner of the narrowing field, cross a stile set into a gate, in the wall on the right-hand edge of the field, some little way short of the end of the field.

- Follow a footpath through woods, soon to cross a stile into a field.
- Keep straight on down the field, with a wall on the right. Where the wall ends, keep ahead for 20 yards to the river bank.
- Follow a sometimes muddy track, with the river on the left, to a gate. Pass through the gate and continue along the track, initially with the river on your left.
- The track leaves the river and becomes enclosed. Follow the track under a railway arch and out to a road.

The 6th Duke of Devonshire was extremely reluctant to allow an extension of the London Midland & Scottish railway line to cross his estate when it was first mooted in the 1850s. His consent was not forthcoming until it was agreed that Sir Joseph Paxton, who was working for the Duke on the redesign of the house and gardens at Chatsworth House, could be engaged to design this part of the route. (Paxton had just finished designing the Crystal Palace in London for the Great Exhibition, which was based upon his earlier design of the greenhouses at Chatsworth.) Paxton's brief included Rowsley Station and four adjoining railway cottages, as well as the railway itself, the whole to be designed tastefully into the landscape (see walk 23 for more of Paxton's work). The line was closed in the Beeching reorganisations of the 1960s.

- Turn right and follow the road through the village of Rowsley. The road climbs out of the village and then becomes an unmade track.
- The trackway soon passes through fields and becomes more open, with views left down over the Derwent valley.
- Follow the track, later becoming enclosed again, for half a mile.

This is an old packhorse trail, crossing a spur between the Wye and Derwent valleys, in use for many hundreds of years until the middle of the last century.

- At a T-junction, barred with two metal horse barriers, turn left along the track into woods.
- Just after leaving the trees, turn right up hill, leaving the main track which starts to descend.
- After a quarter of a mile, turn left at a T-junction.
- Continue ahead, ignoring two tracks joining from the left. After 400 yards, turn right uphill up a broad blue-arrowed track, beside a 'Haddon Estate' signboard.
- The path curves left and soon becomes more open, with a wall joining from the left.
- Turn right and pass through the wall at a gateway. Continue along the track as it winds through more open woodland.

- The path emerges onto a wide unkempt 'ride'. Continue in the same direction, for a while following telephone poles.

- After 400 yards or so the path turns right and follows a wall on the left hand side down to a ladder stile.

- Cross the stile and bear half-left down the hillside.

On your left, just after leaving the wall, the distinctive mound you pass is a tumulus, a burial mound dating from the Bronze Age. Another two would be clearly visible if you were to walk left along the edge of the woods, and across the whole of Chatsworth Park there are many others, including Hob Hurst's House on the other side of the Derwent Valley. The moors above the Derwent have the densest concentration of Bronze Age tombs and house foundations of any part of England outside Dartmoor, and was an area of major settlement four thousand years ago (see walk 3). Unfortunately most of the remains are not on land with public access and so cannot be readily visited.

- Follow a clear bridleway downhill. At the bottom of the slope, bear left with the bridleway, with a wall and trees on your right, and follow the bridleway around to a gate.

- Go through the gate. DO NOT take the broad track ahead up the slope but turn sharp right and follow the wall on your right.

- Follow the wall down to a gate. Do not go through gate but turn left up the slope along a track, keeping a wall on your right hand.

- Where the wall swings right, bear left with the track, aiming just to the left of a barn seen ahead.

- The track leads to a gate 80 yards to the left of the barn. Pass through the gate and follow the track through a band of woods to another gate.

- Cross a step stile beside the gate to enter Chatsworth estate.

Three of the Dukes of Devonshire have made an especial impact upon the Chatsworth Estate: William Cavendish, the 1st Duke, totally rebuilt the original house between 1688 and 1707; the 4th Duke redesigned the park in the 1760s; the 6th Duke built the village of Edensor in the 1860s. You will see the work of these three dukes in the remainder of the walk.

The 4th Duke commissioned the famous landscape architect Launcelot 'Capability' Brown to redesign the park surrounding Chatsworth House in 1762. Brown ripped up much of the natural woodland and meadow, and in its place created sweeping lawns, replanted woods to follow natural contours, and straightened the river. The old public roads that had run east to west across the valley were taken out and a new route (followed today by the B6012) placed more tidily to run north-south down the floor of the valley. Chatsworth Park is a masterpiece of landscape architecture, and epitomises the desire, prevalent amongst the cultured classes in the eighteenth century, for countryside to be tidy and aesthetically pleasing rather than natural. This coincided with a move towards 'Pasturalism' in painting and on the stage, a sentimental eulogising about a sanitised version of country living.

The park was extended in 1823, when land in the south-west were given to the Duke of Rutland, to adjoin his estate at Haddon, in exchange for lands at the northern end of Chatsworth Park, around Baslow.

- Descend quarter-right on a grassy path, aiming just to the left of a stand of trees.

- Continue down through the park, now aiming for the left of a small wood in the valley bottom. The steeple of Edensor church, your destination, is seen ahead.

- Beyond the trees, follow the path across the park, aiming for the steeple of the church.

- Aim to the left of the church steeple. Descend the slope towards the village, with the churchyard on your right hand.

- 50 yards to the left of the churchyard go through a small and easily-missed metal gate and descend an enclosed footpath, then steps, into the village street.

Edensor village is another product of the desire to sanitise the environment. The original village, which housed the workers on the estate, was close to Chatsworth House. When the House was extended in the early nineteenth century, the 6th Duke decided to move the village to a position more convenient for himself, out of sight. Sir Joseph Paxton undertook the work as part of his general redesign of the House and estate, and Edensor was totally rebuilt as ornate cottages, in a deliberate hotch-potch of styles, enclosed by an ornamental gateway. Whilst undoubtedly aesthetically pleasing, it is to be wondered how the estate workers liked the new home so arbitrarily given them. This is epitomised by the Church, rebuilt in Early-English style in 1867 by Gilbert Scott, which is approached from the village square by a splendid-looking flight of steps which would be utterly impractical for an old or infirm villager.

- Turn right and go down through the village, passing the church on your right, and exiting past the gatehouse onto the B6012.

A tower is visible on the wooded slope ahead. This was a hunting tower, and is one of the surviving relics of the old Elizabethan estate that once stood here. It was erected in 158∠ by Bess of Hardwick, who owned Chatsworth and used it as a hunting estate (see walk 13).

- Cross the road and follow the prominent path opposite half-right up the slope.

- Follow the path over the brow of the hill and descend leftwards.

The original Elizabethan property of Chatsworth House was built by Bess of Hardwick and her second husband Sir William Cavendish (see walk 13), but it was

Chatsworth House.

almost totally rebuilt in a classical palladian style between 1686 and 1707 for a later William Cavendish, the 1st Duke of Devonshire. It was to be his main residence and as an outward show of his status and taste. The original redesign was by the architect William Talman, with later work by Thomas Archer, both of whom were heavily influenced by Christopher Wren. State rooms, a private chapel, a magnificent library and a painted hall were all built as part of the initial construction. Opulence as well as the latest fashion in architecture were the order of the day – even many of the exterior window frames were covered in gilt.

Magnificent though the house is, its splendour is greatly enhanced by its setting amidst beautifully designed parklands. Ironically, the 1st Duke never lived to see this in its full glory.

A new north wing, which included an orangery and music gallery was added in the nineteenth century by the 6th Duke. A gallery to display the family collection of sculpture, acquired over many years from around Europe and the Empire, was also added in the early nineteenth century. At the same time, the gardens, laid out as part of the original construction of the house, were added to by Sir Joseph Paxton. Paxton also built a huge fountain, 290 feet high, to honour Czar Nicholas I of Russia who was due to visit Chatsworth. Unfortunately the Czar cancelled his proposed and never saw the fountain. The most outstanding feature of the gardens, the unique Grand Cascade, was part of the original garden designed by Thomas Archer.
Open Easter to 1 November, daily 11.00am-4.30pm. Admission charge.

● Join the road at the bridge over the River Derwent.
The bridge was built in 1758 by James Paine.

● To visit Chatsworth House cross the bridge. Even if you do not intend visiting Chatsworth, it is worth a short detour over the bridge to see Queen Marys Bower. This stands just over the bridge, a few yards to the left of the drive to the house.

Mary Queen of Scots fled to England in May 1568 and became a political liability for her cousin Elizabeth I (see walk 14). Elizabeth could not allow Mary her liberty, and kept her under house arrest for the next sixteen years. For most of that time she was placed in the custody of George Talbot, 6th Earl of Shrewsbury, who had to bear the cost of supporting Mary and her large retinue at his own expense, and bankrupted himself in the process. Shrewsbury provided Mary with every comfort and considerable freedom, and lodged her in three of his northern properties at intervals, Sheffield Castle, Wingfield Manor (see walk 12) and his wife's home, Chatsworth.

The relationship between Shrewsbury and his wife Bess of Hardwick (see walk 13) deteriorated into a bitter feud. Bess was a fiercely independent woman, not prepared to be dominated by any husband, especially her fourth one, and she and Shrewsbury engaged in an ongoing series of public and acrimonious arguments. At one stage Bess even accused her husband of having an affair with Queen Mary. So bad did the situation become between the two that Queen Elizabeth was forced to intervene and demand a reconciliation, after which the feud went underground.

Queen Mary's Bower was a belvedere, an ornamental viewpoint dating from the same era as the original Elizabethan house and the hunting tower on the hill behind. It was built on top of a bronze age tumulus which happened to provide a convenient mound in the right place, and was used for picnics by the owners of the house, as well as serving as a grandstand for any entertainments in the grounds. Mary Queen of Scots would often use this belvedere to while away the long summer days she spent at Chatsworth, and ever since it has been known as Queen Marys Bower. It was left to decay when Chatsworth was redesigned, but was finally restored in 1830.

● To continue the walk return to the Edensor side of the bridge. Walk down the riverbank, keeping the river on your left.

● Walk down the river bank for a mile, until you reach a ruined stone building.

● Just past the building, turn right up the slope and back to the car park.

Swarkestone: the end of the Stuart dream 1745

Distance: 4 miles

Map: OS sheet 128

Start and parking: The walk starts from the cross-roads in the middle of Barrow-upon-Trent (grid ref: 353286), which is just off the A5132, five miles south of Derby. There is ample street parking in Barrow.

Refreshments: Public House and tearoom at Swarkestone.

Historical Background

James II, the last Stuart King of England, went into exile in France after the 'Glorious Revolution' of 1688 (see walk 17). For the next six decades the Jacobite cause, (so named after the Latin name for 'James') was a focus for rebellion against his Hanoverian successors, George I and George II. James tried unsuccessfully for ten years to reconquer his lost throne. After his death three attempts to re-establish the Stuarts were made in the name of his son James 'The Young Pretender'. By 1745 the mantle of the Jacobite cause had fallen to his grandson, Prince Charles Edward, known popularly as Bonnie Prince Charlie.

However, by 1745 the political climate was very different to that in 1688. The French no longer saw the Jacobite cause as a viable tool in their ongoing struggle with England, and their physical support of rebellion was not forthcoming. Opposition to the Hanoverians within England no longer looked to the Stuarts for leadership. Even the Scots, traditionally loyal to the Stuarts, at least in the highlands, no longer saw the restoration of a Stuart king as realistic. When Bonnie Prince Charlie slipped into Scotland in July 1745 his supporters there were appalled and urged him to go home. Charles answered that he was home and set about raising an army.

Although support amongst the leaders of the highland clans was half-hearted, Charles raised sufficient forces to march southwards. An English army was routed at Prestonpans outside Edinburgh and by September Scotland was in Charles' hands. Charles' next aim was London, and his army marched triumphantly southwards through Cumbria and Lancashire, and on 4 December 1745 they reached Derby.

The government was in panic. It had few troops in England and was hastily recalling regiments from the Continent, the militia were unsound, and King George was preparing to flee for Germany. This situation was not recognised by Charles' generals however. They saw themselves as dangerously exposed, with a small army that was hundreds of miles from home in a foreign country which was showing no signs of rising in revolt in support of Charles. They insisted to Charles that the army turn around and return to Scotland. One of the great ironies of history is that Charles, militarily and politically incompetent, may well have been right in his appreciation that had he continued to advance on London victory could have been his. As it was, he was too immature and petulant to prevail over his generals arguments, and the order to retreat was given. Four months later, the Jacobite cause ended for ever at Culloden.

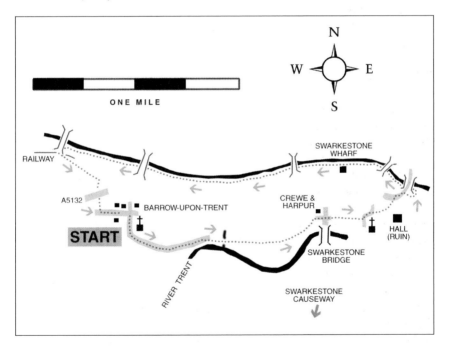

The Walk

This walk goes along the River Trent to Swarkestone bridge, the most southerly point reached by the Jacobite army. It then passes the remains of Swarkestone Hall, which saw service in the Civil War, and returns along the Trent & Mersey Canal.

- From the cross roads in the middle of Barrow-upon-Trent, go down Church Lane. Pass 'Hall Park' on your left and 30 yards later look out for a 'pinfold' on the right (behind a white gate and now looking at first glance like the wall to a garden).

A pinfold was a compound for stray livestock, a number of which can be seen across Derbyshire. A town official was appointed to round up any stray sheep or cattle that were loose in the town and impound them in a pinfold until their owners paid a fine.

- Follow the lane as it curves left around the church and graveyard.
- Continue along the lane, passing houses on the left and a pumping station on the right.
- The lane is joined by the River Trent on your right hand side. Where the lane ends at the entrance to an ivy-covered cottage (Crow Trees) keep ahead along a footpath on the bank of the river.
- Follow the enclosed footpath over a plank footbridge into a field.
- Continue ahead along the field edge, with the river on your right hand.
- Pass through a gateway into the next field. Leave the river bank and go half-left across the field, towards the right side of a small wood in mid-field.
- Continue towards the wood, passing under telegraph wires, 25 yards short of the wood the path swings right and follows the boundary of the wood in a shallow curve, keeping the trees some 25 yards away to the left.
- The path leads to a stile in a wire fence, 20 yards to the right of the top left-hand corner of the field. Cross the stile and keep ahead across a rough paddock to a gap in the hedge on the far side.
- Go through the gap and keep ahead, now with the hedge on your left hand, to reach a cross track.

Ahead of you is Swarkestone Bridge. There has been mention of a bridge here since at least 1204, when it was built by the Prior of Repton Priory to avoid the use of a dangerous ford across the fast flowing Trent. In 1327 a surveyor was appointed by the priory to maintain the bridge and a chapel which was built on the southern end, with a priest delegated to collect both prayers and tolls from travellers. In 1713 chains were fitted under the arches to prevent travellers sneaking under the bridge in boats to avoid paying the toll. The medieval bridge was finally swept away by flood waters in 1801, and the bridge you see today was built in its stead.

On the morning of 5 December 1745 a detachment of 70 men, the advance guard of Bonnie Prince Charles' army, arrived to hold the bridge. The River Trent is the last natural frontier between here and London, a mere 120 miles south. Once across this narrow bridge and the mile long causeway beyond it, there was no natural defensive line at which to halt the advance of the Scots army.

The Jacobite army consisted of two main groups. There were clan regiments, professional soldiers in the pay of a local lord, with a degree of military training and

Swarkestone Bridge, the turning point for the Jacobite army.

reasonably modern weapons. These accounted for about half of Charles' army. Then there were the feudal brigades, mostly retainers and tenants whose land tenure obliged them to fight for their lord. These men fought, with varying degrees of enthusiasm, out of loyalty to their clan rather than any belief in the Stuart cause. These brigades had no form of military drill or training and displayed a wide range of weaponry: the chiefs and their immediate tenants would be armed with muskets, pistols, broadswords (the dreaded Scottish claymore) and small shields, whilst the poorest tenants may have had as little as a dagger or a pitchfork. The Jacobite army had few cavalry, and these were used for escort duty and as messengers.

Due to the lack of training of highland armies, their battle tactic was simple in the extreme: move to within a thirty or so yards of the enemy, preferably uphill of him, fire all available muskets, and then charge downhill, screaming ferociously and attempting to hit any available target with a broadsword. The effectiveness of this tactic should not be underestimated. It had a terrifying psychological impact and had routed an English army at Prestonpans in ten minutes flat. The Scots, viewed anyway as foreign barbarians, had an awesome military reputation and were much feared.

- Turn left along the cross track for 30 yards to reach a stile by a metal field gate.
- Cross the stile and keep ahead, to follow a drive out to a lane.
- Turn right along the lane to reach the main road beside the Crewe and Harpur public house, at the foot of Swarkestone bridge.

The Crewe and Harpur is an old coaching inn, built as a staging point on the main road to London. It dates from the second half of the eighteenth century, a few years after the Jacobites retreated.

● Cross the road onto a path opposite. DO NOT keep ahead down the clear path along the river bank, but stay left with a wall immediately on your left hand.

It is worthwhile detouring to the river bank for a view of Swarkestone Causeway, a stone embankment built to carry the main road for nearly a mile across the flood plain of the River Trent. This view has altered little since 1745, when the Scots arrived on this spot and looked over into lowland England.

The Scottish advance guard that were sent to hold Swarkestone Bridge were from the disciplined and professional clan regiments. They had marched on foot from Derby, and were under strict orders to behave respectfully to the local population (Charles after all saw the locals as his subjects, to be liberated from Hanoverian oppression). They encamped here on this river bank, with pickets at the far end of the causeway to give warning of any advancing English army.

They remained here for a day and a night, whilst their higher command were in Exeter House in Derby, engaging in protracted and acrimonious debate about the future of the campaign. At the end of that time they were ordered to return to their regiment. Not a shot had been fired.

● Follow the left-hand wall into an enclosed path between gardens, to a stile in a field (at one point the path seems to run through a garden).

● Cross the stile and continue along the edge of the field, with a fence and hedge on your right hand.

● Cross another stile and continue ahead, passing allotments and a barn on your left, to reach a lane opposite the church of St James'.

● Turn left to follow the churchyard wall around. Where the lane leaves the wall, continue to follow the wall around, to a stile on the left. opposite the rear gate into the churchyard.

● Cross the stile and turn half-left across the field, aiming to the left of a line of trees in midfield, to a stile by a farm signpost.

The elaborate gateway to the right is all that remains of Swarkestone Hall. Whether this building was put up as a summer house, a gatehouse or a pavilion is unknown. The Hall itself stood just south of here, between the gatehouse and the river, roughly where the farm now stands. It was ancestral home of the Harpur family for many centuries. In 1642, at the start of the Civil War Sir John Harpur fortified the Hall to act as a stronghold from which to hold the strategically important Swarkestone Bridge. Harpur was an ardent Royalist, and was supporting an earlier Charles Stuart, namely Charles I, great-grandfather of Bonnie Prince Charlie. Harpur's forces were defeated in a sharp skirmish with Parliamentarian forces led by Colonel Hastings, and the Hall occupied by the Parliamentarians for the rest of the war, after which it was totally demolished.

After the restoration of the monarchy in 1660 the Harpur family fortunes revived, and the following century they bought nearby Calke Park and built the present Calke Abbey as the family home (see walk 24).

The family tombs of the Harpurs are in St James' Church.

- Cross the stile and turn right along the main road for 250 yards. Just before the bridge, turn right and go down a short enclosed path to the tow-path.

- Turn left under the bridge and go along the tow-path, with the canal on your right.

- In 300 yards pass a sluice on your left, and shortly after go under the railway.

- At the next bridge in 150 yards, climb up to cross a lane. Continue ahead along the side of Swarkestone Lock, with the keepers cottage on the left. Continue ahead along the canal.

- In 300 yards pass a wharf with a crane and warehouse. Keep straight on.

This 93-mile long canal connects the Trent with the Mersey. A milestone here indicates that Preston Brook on the Mersey is 86 miles to the west, whilst Shardlow (see walk 19), a major port on the canal and only one mile from its confluence with the Rivers Trent and Derwent, is 6 miles to the east. Canals were not only used to provide long distance communications, but served the countryside they travelled through. The wharf and warehouse here are a reminder of the days when inland ports lined the canals, loading the produce of both the local farms and local factories onto narrow boats for shipment across the country.

- Continue along the canal for a mile and a half, passing under two road bridges. At the third bridge, a smaller redbrick one carrying a farm track, go up onto an unmade track.

- Turn left and in 20 yards cross the railway by way of a bridge.

- Follow the track for 100 yards to a pair of gates. Go over a stile beside the left-hand gate.

- Cross the field quarter-left, aiming for a gate in the hedge between two trees.

- Go through the gate and bear half-right across the next field, to a gap and farm bridge in the bottom right-hand corner of the field.

- Cross the bridge and go ahead down the next long field, aiming for a metal field gate in the bottom hedge.

- Carefully cross the road (A5132) to a Footpath Sign beside brown wooden gates opposite. Go along the footpath, initially with a hedge on the right and link-fence on the left.

- Emerge into a suburban road. Turn left back to the cross-roads you started at.

Shardlow: canal mania in the eighteenth century

Distance: 3 miles

Map: OS sheet 129

Start and parking: The walk starts from the Shardlow Wharf car park (grid ref: 445305). Shardlow is on the A6, 7 miles east of Derby. The car park is clearly marked up Wilne Lane, from the main A6 through the village.

Refreshments: Public houses and shop in Shardlow.

Historical Background

For the industrial revolution to succeed, it was necessary for there to be a corresponding revolution in transport. The large scale production of goods needed not only new technology and new ways of organising labour, but also the means to move increasing quantities of raw materials and finished goods quickly and cheaply around the country. In the mid-eighteenth century these means did not exist apart from around the coast. Rivers were often obstructed by weirs and fishpools, and very few could provide for the long-distance haulage of goods. Roads were of very poor quality, rutted and unsurfaced. Although the growth of the turnpikes – essentially private toll roads reasonably well maintained – improved the situation for passenger traffic, they were unsuitable for moving large volumes of goods. In Derbyshire freight transport still relied upon the packhorse, up to a hundred animals in a line, transporting goods slowly and laboriously along narrow tracks.

In 1759 a revolution in transport occurred. Francis Egerton, 2nd Duke of Bridgewater, tired of London society and disappointed in love, threw his energies into constructing a canal to connect his coalmines in Worsley to nearby Manchester. To do this Bridgewater employed James Brindley, a millwright with no formal education, who brought a natural genius to the task of civil engineering, overcame tremendous natural obstacles, and in 1761 opened the first commercial canal in England.

The success of the canal as a means of moving heavy goods quickly and cheaply was immediately apparent, and the next 60 years saw canals being opened the length and breadth of Britain, in such numbers that it was described as 'canal mania'. Although the heyday of the canals was soon over, superseded by the invention of the railway, they revolutionised transport in Britain. Canals were initially constructed by the producers of raw materials, especially owners of mines and collieries, but soon were used and extended by inland manufacturers to move their finished goods to a wider market. In the process, inland ports grew up for the loading and unloading of goods, and these in turn became new centres for trade. One of the best preserved of these inland ports is Shardlow.

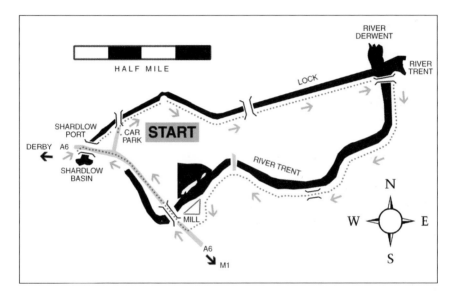

The Walk

This short walk starts in Shardlow, one of the best preserved canal ports in England. It goes along the Trent & Mersey Canal, which displays many features typical of eighteenth-century canals, and returns along the River Trent.

● Go out of the car park back to the road and turn right for 100 yards, to reach a bridge over the canal.

● Do not cross the bridge but turn left down steps onto the tow-path.
This canal connects the River Trent with the River Mersey, and is now called, somewhat obviously, the Trent and Mersey Canal. When it was opened however it was called by the grander name of the Grand Trunk Canal, since it enabled the transportation of goods from the east of England to the west. In the 1760s the pottery towns of Staffordshire suffered serious transport difficulties. Clay had to be brought into the Potteries by packhorse from Liverpool. Flint was carried down the River

Trent from Hull by riverboat, and then transferred to packhorse for the rest of its journey. Finished pottery was taken by packhorse to the River Trent or the River Severn. Costs and breakages were high.

In 1765 Josiah Wedgewood started the process necessary to build a canal. Firstly it was necessary to have an Act of Parliament passed, giving the right for the compulsory purchase of the land needed. Next a joint stock company had to be raised, to finance the building, which would require far more capital than any previous canal. Eventually Wedgewood got sufficient backers, including the Duke of Bridgewater, to finance the new canal. Finally the canal had to be actually built and James Brindley, engineer to the Duke of Bridgewater, was employed for this task.

The canal was opened in 1777, going through the potteries and the salt-mining area of Cheshire, connecting the Mersey and the port of Liverpool to the Trent and hence the Humber and the port of Hull. Brindley, worn out by his efforts, died before this canal, his masterpiece, was completed.

● Turn right and walk under the bridge. Continue along the tow-path, with the canal on your left.

● In 150 yards pass the entrance to a mooring area for narrow boats.

Just before the entrance to the mooring area, note the spur of canal in front of the house opposite, a private parking bay for a 'narrow boat'. Although the canal was originally built to allow for the long-distance transportation of heavy goods, once it existed use was made of it along its whole length. The canal passed through open agricultural land as well as manufacturing and mining centres, and local farmers would construct small private mooring areas, to allow them to put their produce onto

The inland port of Shardlow.

passing barges to be transported to market. The mooring area here is the successor to those private farm 'docks', just as todays narrow boat is the successor of the working barges. It is built just wide enough to pass through the canal locks.

● Continue along the tow-path, shortly passing under a bridge ('No. 1').

● Pass the Derwent Mouth Lock.

There are 76 locks along the canal, necessary to allow barges to climb up out of the Mersey valley and then drop down again into the Trent. Of these, 69 are of the original, narrow, design, just wide enough to accommodate one barge or narrow boat at a time. The remaining seven, mainly at this the eastern end of the canal, are wide locks, able to take two barges abreast, thereby speeding up the process of going up and down a lock. Note the sluice off to the left of the Lock; this is an overflow drainage channel which enables the flow of water along the canal to be regulated.

● A mile after leaving Shardlow, you come to the junction of the Rivers Trent and Derwent, and the Trent & Mersey Canal.

This is the eastern end of the Trent & Mersey Canal, which goes for 93 miles, in a huge arc southwards into the Potteries of Staffordshire before going north again to the Mersey.

● Cross the River Trent by a long footbridge, built in the style of a packhorse bridge.

● At the end of the bridge turn right and follow a broad surfaced path alongside the River Trent, with the river on your right.

● After 1,000 yards the surfaced path swings left, away from the river, to a concrete bridge. Leave the path at this point and continue on a fainter footpath along the river bank.

● Shortly after leaving the surfaced path, cross a concrete bridge over a drainage ditch. Continue along the river bank.

At this point, the footpath as shown on the OS map leaves the river and crosses the field. However, at the time of writing it has been 'temporally' diverted whilst a quarry is dug. The instructions are for the diverted route, which I suspect will become permanent.

● Follow the river bank, passing under a sewage pipe that crosses the river.

● On reaching the walls of an ex-mill, opposite the entrance to Shardlow Marina, turn left. Keeping the wall close on your right-hand, follow the building around to reach a stile beside a field gate.

● Cross the stile and go out onto the A6.

● Turn right and walk along the surprisingly un-busy A6, crossing a bridge and following the road into Shardlow.

● Pass the Navigation Inn and Wilne Lane on the right and follow the A6 to reach the canal.

● Cross the bridge and look left.

What is now the Heritage Centre was once a farriers shop. Barges were for the most part drawn by horses, who therefore required all the services associated with horses. The farrier here supplied corn and forage: on the opposite side of the bridge and canal was a blacksmiths, to shoe the horses and repair and replace tackle. Trades traditionally associated with the countryside and village life migrated to the canal-side to serve the new sources of work.

The Clock Warehouse public house was, as its name suggests, originally a warehouse. A spur of the canal can still be seen to run into the warehouse through an arch. Barges would be brought along the main canal, pulled up the spur into the warehouse, where goods could be loaded onto them directly from storage.

Agricultural produce from the surrounding area, and goods manufactured in nearby Derby, were brought by road to Shardlow to be loaded onto barges and transported to markets across the rest of the country. Indeed, Shardlow was the port from which Derby textiles departed for markets across the whole world.

Before the canal was built, Shardlow had been on the limit of navigation on the River Trent, although dredging gave intermittent access as far as Burton. As such, Shardlow became an important river port, with traffic along the River Trent dominated by Leonard Fosbrooke, a wealthy local trader who built Shardlow Hall as his home in 1684. With the creation of the canal, Shardlow became one of the major inland ports in England, primarily serving Derby and Burton. Many merchants based themselves in Shardlow and made their fortunes here, and evidence of this can still be seen in the numerous grand Georgian houses that are dotted around the village.

● Shardlow Hall and village centre are half a mile further along the A6. To continue with the walk, return to the bridge.

● Cross the bridge and at the far end turn left down onto the tow-path.

● Go along the tow-path, with the canal on the left.

On the opposite bank of the canal are all the facilities normally seen in a coastal port. There is a boatyard, for building and repairing narrow boats, only one now but in its heyday there were several boatyards here in Shardlow. Nearby is a Chandlers, a supplier of all the spare parts necessary for a boat, ropes, tackle, ships lamps. There was once even a small sailmakers here in Shardlow, now long gone: although most barges relied upon horses for their motive power, some were fitted with a mast and sail with which to take advantage of wind power when it was available.

As well as the service industry necessary to support a working water-borne transport, there are many warehouses behind the wharves that line the opposite bank. When it was a working port, these wharves had cranes and gantries, to enable goods to be unloaded. The warehouses contained goods for export from the area, and also housed imports, as trade through Shardlow was two-way: produce from around the world came into Britain through Liverpool and Hull, and was transported by barge to Shardlow before being taken into Derby for sale.

- Continue along the tow-path, to a bridge, opposite the New Inn.
- Go up steps on the side of the bridge to reach a road.
- Turn right for 100 yards back to the car park.

Cromford, 'Cradle of the Industrial Revolution'.

Distance: 5 miles

Map: OS sheet 119

Start and parking: Pay & display car park and picnic area, opposite Cromford Old Mill in Cromford, (grid ref: 300570). Upon entering Cromford along the A6, follow signs for 'Station' and 'Long Stay Car Park'. The car park is on the right just after the Mill, 300 yards from the A6.

Refreshments: Shops, tearoom and public houses in Cromford: seasonal tearoom at High Peak Junction.

Historical Background

Sir Richard Arkwright is rightly seen as the father of the Industrial Revolution. He developed new mechanised methods of producing cotton, and in doing so changed the industrial landscape forever. Prior to Arkwright, manufacturing had largely been done at home or in small workshops, by workers who often divided their time between the workbench and the fields. Arkwright's inventions demanded the factory and with it the industrial town and a dedicated work force. This process started in Cromford, which is a perfect example of the development of a factory town, and which helped to give Derbyshire the title of 'The cradle of the Industrial Revolution'.

Before mechanisation, the spinning of cotton had always been done by hand, and required skilled operators. Arkwright's Water Frame not only greatly increased the speed of spinning and therefore the volume of cotton produced, but it also had the great advantage that it could be operated by young people with very little training. However, the size of the machinery and its need for a power source meant it could no longer be used in the home, but had to be housed in a specially constructed factory.

At first the labour force was found amongst the local farming and mining community, but as production increased, workers were imported from outside the area. A whole town was constructed to house them, rows of cottages, a hotel and a chapel, and the pattern for later industrial towns emerged.

The success of the factory system in turn stimulated demand for more efficient communications, leading Arkwright and other industrialists who had come into the area to invest in building firstly the Cromford Canal and subsequently the High Peak Railway.

Unlike many later industrialists, Arkwright was an enlightened employer: the dwellings he built were good quality, the facilities provided by the town excellent, and generous incentives provided both for his factory workers and for town traders to maximise their potential. Arkwright lived in the town he had effectively created, initially in a house adjoining his factory, but later building the palatial Willersley Castle as a home suitable for a modern day industrial baron.

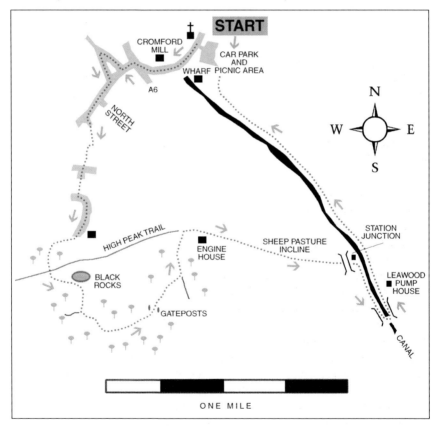

The Walk

This walk goes past Arkwright's original mill and through the town he built to

**house his workers, climbs up to Black Rocks, and passes through wooded hills
before returning along the Cromford Canal.**

● Return to the car park entrance, noting the canal on your left and, at the car
park entrance, passing the canal wharf and associated buildings.

*This is Cromford Wharf, once a busy port for both freight and passengers. After
Richard Arkwright had built the world's first water-powered cotton-spinning mill at
Cromford in 1771, he required vastly improved communications to bring raw
materials to his factory and take finished textiles from it. The first stage of this was
the building of a fourteen-and-a-half mile long canal between Cromford and the
River Erewash at Langley Mill, where the canal in turn connected with Trent Canal
and thus with the national canal network. The Cromford Canal was designed by
William Jessop, and opened in 1793. The canal remained a vital artery for Cromford
for seventy years, until made redundant by the building of the London-Manchester
Railway in 1867, which passed through Cromford.*

*In 1900 the canal was cut off from the main national canal network when the
Butterley Tunnel collapsed. This effectively marked the end of the canal as a working
communications route, and although it continued to be used for purely local traffic,
it was finally closed in 1944. Today only six miles of the canal has any water in it,
and it is too silted up to be navigable.*

● At the car park entrance, cross the road and go a few yards to your right, to
St Marys Church.

*This has been the parish church of Cromford since 1797, but it was built by Richard
Arkwright as the private chapel of his estate. His mansion, Willersley Castle, lies
behind the church, reached by a private drive. Arkwright is buried within this
church.*

● With your back to the church turn right along the road towards Cromford,
re-passing the entrance of the car park. Stay on the right-hand side of the
road, where there is a pavement. In 100 yards pass the entrance to Cromford
Old Mill.

*Machines such as the 'Spinning Jenny', invented by James Hargreaves in 1764, had
speeded up the production of cotton, but still required skilled operators. Richard
Arkwright, the son of a Preston tailor, looked for a way of making the production
process faster and removing its reliance upon a skilled workforce. Arkwright worked
with John Kay, building upon Kay's work and in 1868 perfecting a roller-driven
frame for spinning textiles.*

*Power was the limiting factor as to how fast the machine could work. After
initially using horses, Arkwright adapted his machine to be driven by water power,
and in 1768 the Water Frame was born as a way of mechanising the process of
spinning. Lacking the capital to develop his invention alone, Arkwright went into
partnership with Samuel Need and Jedediah Strutt (see walk 21) and with their
money behind him set about developing a water-powered mill. Water power from*

Richard Arkwright's planned town of Cromford.

Bonsall Brook was initially used to drive machinery in the first mill, which he opened on this spot in 1771. The water power from the stream soon proved insufficient, and water from Cromford Sough was soon diverted into the mill to provide a more efficient power source.

The original mill was a five story building, well lit by windows along its whole length, although it was thought prudent not to put any windows at ground floor level. This was partly to stop any spying by rivals, but also to make the mill defensible should there be any trouble, either from disgruntled workers or from those opposed to the new process of mechanisation. This mill was used exclusively for spinning, but Arkwright also set about mechanising all the other parts of the textile production process. Invention followed invention and in 1777 Arkwright built a second mill on the Cromford site, considerably larger than the first, housing mechanised carding and cleaning processes as well as spinning. At the same time the water supply necessary to power the mills was increased, by building an aqueduct to bring water in to drive two huge waterwheels.

The Cromford Old Mill site contained not only the two mills, but also warehouses and workshops. Arkwright originally lived behind the mill, in Rock House, before building nearby Willersley Castle as a more grandiose home. Arkwright went on to build further mills at Bakewell, Cressbrook and Matlock.

Cromford Mill is owned by the Arkwright Society, who are in the process of restoring the site. It is open to the public every day except Christmas Day, access free.

● Follow the road up to traffic lights at the A6.

The aqueduct you pass was built in 1821 to carry water from Cromford Sough to drive the wheel in Cromford Mill. A 'sough' is a horizontal drainage channel, dug from the lower levels of a mine to drain flood water out of the workings. This sough was dug in 1631, and drained the lead mines at Wirksworth, on the hills above Cromford.

- Cross the A6 by the traffic island at the lights and turn left into the village of Cromford.

- Before reaching the Greyhound Hotel, seen clearly on the right, turn right up a narrow lane on the right, soon passing the Boat Inn on the left and the Post Office on the right. Shortly there is a fine view on the left over the mill pond.

- At a T-junction with a more major road, turn left.

Note Cromford Garage on the junction to your right, built into an old church building.

- 30 yards down the road, pass a working water wheel on your left, on the edge of the mill pond.

This type of wheel was typical of those used to drive the mills of Arkwright's day.

- Continue down the road, with the mill pond on your left, passing a school and chapel on your right, to reach the main road at a T-junction with Market Place.

- Turn right up 'The Hill', passing the Bell Inn on your left.

- The Bell stands on the corner with North Street.

North Street contains a terrace of three-storey dwellings, that front directly onto the street, built in 1776 by Richard Arkwright to house mill workers as part of his overall development of Cromford as a mill town. It was the first planned street in Derbyshire, and both the housing and their environment were designed to a high standard rarely seen previously.

- Continue up The Hill, passing another terrace of original workers cottages on the left. At the end of the cottages, by a bus stop, turn left into Bedehouse Lane.

- After 10 yards, turn right uphill, following the lane.

- After a further 50 yards, turn right up a tarmaced cycle track.

- Follow the path uphill. Follow the path as it turns right and immediately left again, in front of almshouses, and follow the path out to reach a quiet suburban road.

These almshouses were built in the 17th century and pre-date Arkwright's development of Cromford, being provided by the parish to house its poor.

- Cross slightly right over the road and continue up an enclosed drive.

- At the entrance to a bungalow (no. 38) continue straight on up a narrow tarmaced footpath.

- Pass through a squeeze stile and turn left along a wider drive. Watch out for occasional cars on this drive.

- Follow the drive as it bends right through a metal field gate, and then bends left, continuing to climb.

- Where the drive levels out, do not turn right (signposted 'Black Rocks and High Peak Trail') but continue straight on towards a small terrace of houses seen ahead.

- At the houses, turn right through a pedestrian gate into a field. Walk down the field, continuing the same line of advance and keeping the wall on your left, towards a quarry seen in front.

There are fine views ahead, over Cromford and up the Derwent Valley towards Matlock. The Heights of Abraham with its cable car can be seen on the left, the nineteenth-century folly Riber Castle on the hills to the right, with the rocky outcrop of High Tor between.

- At the corner of the field, climb through a gap in the wall ahead.

- DO NOT turn downhill, but keep straight on across the top of an open area, and continue the same line of advance along a path entering woods.

- Ascend with the path through trees. Curve left and pass a car park off to your right.

- Climb up some steps, soon with a wall on your left, to reach a road at the corner of a car park.

- Turn left through a gate. Do not turn sharp left onto the High Peak Trail, but go straight on up a broad waymarked track to Black Rocks.

(If you wish to take a short cut, you can turn left along the High Peak Trail. This is a gentler walk, and cuts a half mile off the walk.)

- Black Rocks are an outcrop of Millstone grit, popular with climbers. It is an easy scramble up the side to reach the top of the rocks, and you will be amply rewarded with magnificent views.

The planned development of Cromford can clearly be seen from Black Rocks. To the left is the chimney of Masson Mill, to the right in the dip Cromford Old Mill, both owned by Arkwright. In the foreground are the streets of old Cromford which housed the workers in the mills, built to a plan, not developing organically. On the hillside beyond and dominating the town is Willersley Castle, a beautifully symmetrical mansion built of local stone. This was to be Arkwright's crowning glory, a palace fit for the new lord of the manor, but Arkwright died before it was completed.

For those who have decided against going up Black Rocks, a slightly less dramatic view of the same scene can be obtained from the High Peak Trail later on.

- From the bottom of the rocks, where the slope levels out, follow the waymarked path into trees, bearing left with the rocks on your left.

- Follow the waymarked path uphill, now occasionally stepped, to a cross track.

- Turn left along the cross track. The path soon levels out.

- At a T-junction follow the path to the right, up wooden steps.

- At the top of the steps, at a fork, DO NOT take the right hand path marked with yellow arrows, but fork left, past a yellow-topped post. Curve left with the path and follow it as it descends through trees and bracken.

- The path descends to a cross-track, at a yellow-topped post. Here turn left and pass through a wall at ruined stone gateposts.

- Immediately through the gateposts, keep straight ahead, now following blue-topped posts slightly uphill.

- The path broadened out and soon starts to gently descend. Blue-topped posts at intervals show you are on the right route.

- Eventually you reach a T-junction, where turn left, still following blue-topped posts.

- Pass a fallen wall on your left and keep ahead, to descend the path on wooden steps to reach the High Peak Trail (the short cut missing Black Rocks rejoins the main walk here).

The High Peak Trail follows the course of the Cromford & High Peak Railway, built in 1830 to connect the Peak Forest Canal with the Cromford Canal. This connecting link was originally conceived as also being a canal, but the engineering difficulties were too great and the cost too high, and so it was decided to construct a railway instead. The trackway runs for 33 miles, and climbs 990 feet. When it was opened wagons were pulled along the flat sections of the track by horses, and dragged up the steep inclines by fixed steam engines. The horses were soon replaced by mobile steam trains, but even then it took 16 hours to travel the 33 miles of track.

The expected volume of trade did not materialise, and the railway was in financial difficulties from its opening. It was saved by the building of the London to Manchester railway down the nearby Derwent Valley in 1867. The High Peak Railway was extended by half a mile to connect with this line and thus to the national network. At the same time, demand for limestone was increasing, and instead of using the railway to transport stone from afar, new quarries were opened along the High Peak line to service this growing need. The line remained in use until 1967.

- Turn right along the High Peak Trail. Within 20 yards pass the Sheep Pasture engine house on your right.

This engine house was opened in 1830. It contained a stationary steam winding engine built by the Butterley Company and was used to pull trains up the 1:8 incline 1320 yards long, leading up from the High Peak junction. Wagons were hauled up on a continuous wire rope, with descending trucks usually balanced by ascending ones.

Just past the engine house, at the top of the incline, note a circular, trenched, platform: this was used to support a horizontal pulley and gearing wheels, around which the winching cable passed.

● Descend the steep Sheep Pasture Incline on the High Peak Trail.

If you look back after about quarter of a mile you will be able to fully appreciate the difficulty of pulling laden trains up this incline, and the engineering feat required to overcome this.

● After half a mile, just before the tunnel, look out for a pit on your right.

This was a catch pit, designed to catch runaway wagons and installed in 1888, after two wagons broke loose on the incline and careered down the slope and across both the canal and the railway before coming to rest. Points were set to automatically deflect any wagon descending too fast, into the catch pit.

● Pass under the A6 by a tunnel. Pass a short section of original rail (possibly the oldest piece of rail still in its original position in the world), and a restored guards van from the Cromford Railway, to reach the Cromford Canal at Station Junction, with an information office in the old stationmasters office.

Arkwright and other local industrialists had an ever-increasing demand for improved communication into Cromford. The Cromford Canal had been opened in 1793, followed in 1820 by the Belper to Matlock Turnpike. The High Peak Railway had been opened in 1830, but immediately posed the need for an interconnection with the canal. Textiles, Coal, iron and limestone as well as passengers were carried.

● Do not cross the canal but turn right along it.

● After 200 yards pass a warehouse and covered wharf.

This was the actual terminus of the High Peak Railway. At this point goods were interchanged between canal barge and railway.

● Follow the track along the side of the warehouse, passing under the height gauge for ensuring that railway wagons were not overloaded.

● 60 yards past the warehouse, turn left at white railings to regain the canal bank, opposite a pumping house and with a turning circle for canal barges on your left.

● Continue along the canal tow-path. In 200 yards cross the aqueduct which carried the canal over the River Derwent.

The Wigwall aqueduct is 600 yards long and crosses the River Derwent on three arches. It was necessary in order to keep the flow of the canal on an even level.

● Turn left across the canal via a swing footbridge, and turn left again to walk back up the opposite bank of the canal, recrossing the aqueduct.

● In 100 yards pass the pumping house on your left.

The Leawood pump house was opened in 1849, to pump water from the River Derwent into the canal in times of water shortage. For this task it used a single-action beam engine, capable of lifting 5 tons of water a minute, up to a height of 30 feet.

● Continue along the canal, soon passing the station buildings on the opposite bank.

● Continue along the tow-path, with the canal on your left, for a mile.

Note that the canal is now heavily silted, and reduced to only a fraction of its working depth. Note too as you walk along how the progressive developments of communication connecting Cromford with the rich markets of the South, – canal, A6 which runs along the route of the old turnpike, and railway – run side by side through the Derwent gorge.

● After a mile the car park is reached on your right.

Belper: from Saxon village to industrial town

Distance: 5.5 miles

Map: OS sheet 119

Start and parking: The walk starts at the Parish Church of St Peter, just off Green Lane, in the middle of Belper (grid ref: 351477). Belper is on the A6, 10 miles north of Derby. There are numerous car parks in Belper: park in whichever is most convenient.

Refreshments: Shops, cafés and public houses in Belper; public houses at Milford.

Historical Background

There has been a village on the site of Belper since Saxon times, listed in the Domesday Book as 'Beau Repaire', the 'Beautiful Retreat'. The original village was a handful of houses and a small church, clustered around a village green. The estate of Beau Repaire was given by William the Conqueror to the De Ferrers family, part of their reward for their support in the Norman Conquest. The De Ferrers used the estate for recreational hunting, creating a deer enclosure, Belper Park, around the village. They also built a hunting lodge and also a small chapel for their foresters.

Coal and iron are present in the area, and were worked on a small scale in little workshops attached to the houses around the village green. By 1260 Belper, as the village was now known, was becoming the centre of a domestic industry making nails, used mainly for shoeing horses. Over the next few centuries Belper consolidated its position as a major nail producing area. It was still however only a small village, surrounded by fields, with a population of only 550 or so right up until 1770.

In 1771 Richard Arkwright went into partnership with two rich manufacturers in Nottingham, Samuel Need and Jedediah Strutt, to develop water-powered mills in the Derbyshire valleys (see walk 20). When the partnership was dissolved in 1781, Strutt kept the mills built in Belper and Milford just to the south, and set about building an industrial empire. Belper

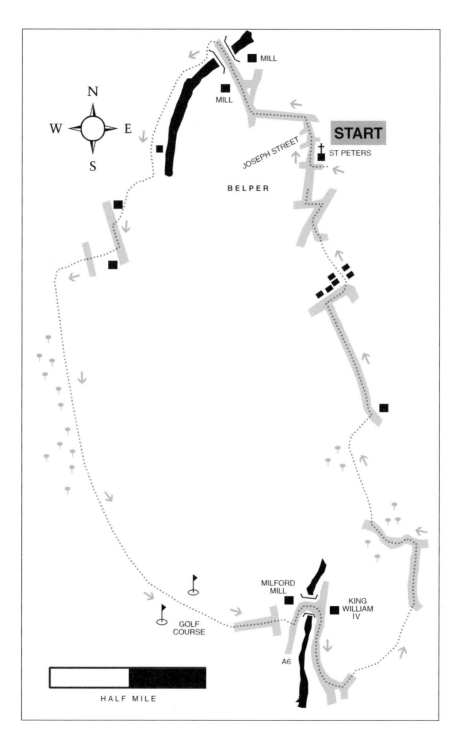

N
W E
S

MILL

MILL

START

JOSEPH STREET   ST PETERS

BELPER

MILFORD
MILL

KING
WILLIAM
IV

A6

GOLF
COURSE

HALF MILE

rapidly became his foremost mill, requiring an ever-growing workforce, and the small village in a sleepy rural valley changed forever. By 1801 the population of Belper had risen to 4,500, and by 1840 it was 10,000, the biggest town in the county, with threequarters of the workforce employed in the mill.

The Strutts, Jedediah and later his son William, were staunchly Christian and felt a duty to look after their workers, body and soul. They built good quality houses for their employees, churches and chapels, a swimming bath and a reading room. They encouraged Sunday school for the children, built a grammar school in Belper, and pioneered day-release classes for the apprentices in their mills. The town of Belper as it is today owes much to the foundations laid down 150 years ago.

The Walk

This walk goes through historic Belper, passing sites that chart its development from Saxon times to Victorian. It then goes down the beautiful Derwent Valley to Milford Mill before returning over the hills to Belper again.

● Stand with your back to the main doors of St Peter's Church.

You are at the historic centre of Belper. The original village green was just to the back of St Peters, behind you. Around the village green were the crude dwellings of the villagers, and surrounding the village were the huge open fields where the villagers worked the land of their lord and grew their own crops. Looking down the hill from where the steps of St Peters are now you would have seen fields stretching down the slope to the river beyond. After the Norman Conquest the new owners of the land, the De Ferrers family, encouraged the development of an iron-working industry, with workshops attached to some of the houses where nails were made, exploiting local reserves of coal and iron.

The De Ferrers also extended the original Saxon church, which became the foundation of St Peters. The present church was heavily restored in Victorian times, although fragments of the Norman original can still be found.

● With your back to the main doors, descend the steps in front of you and go down a grassy, tree-lined drive through the graveyard to iron gates. (The Congregational Church is visible just to your right).

● Turn right along the road (Church Lane) for 10 yards, then turn right into Green Lane.

● Go along Green Lane, passing Belper Congregational Church on your right, and in 100 yards reaching Joseph Street on your left.

The Strutt family were strict Unitarians, and built several chapels in Belper, which they actively encouraged their workers to attend. The chapels also ran Sunday schools for the workers children. The Congregational Church is on the site of one such chapel.

● Turn left down Joseph Street for 40 yards, to see the Nailshop on the right.

Until the middle of the eighteenth century Belper's population was only about 550 people, most still engaged in agriculture but with a number of small nailshops in the gardens of houses. The nailshop here in Joseph Street is one of the last surviving shops from that era, and the best preserved. Shops like this were owned and worked by a single family, who passed their manufacturing skills down from generation to generation. It was this skill-base that was to provide the foundation for Belper's expansion as an industrial town. This shop was on the outskirts of the village, with open fields beyond it stretching down to the river bank.

● Return to Green Lane and turn left to resume your previous direction. In a hundred yards or so you will pass George Street on your left, and then almost immediately Short Row on your right.

Jedediah Strutt built his first cotton mill in Belper in 1773, attracted to the village by the presence of skilled artisan workers and the fast-flowing River Derwent which would power his new factory. The advantage of the factory system to the entrepreneurs of the day was that it only required a few skilled workers to maintain the machinery, whilst the bulk of the work could be done by unskilled labour requiring little training. Initially the labour was recruited locally, but soon the need for a larger workforce necessitated workers being attracted into the area from far afield. By 1801 the population had increased to 4,500.

Strutt built street after street of small cottages to house his workforce. The cottages in Short Row date from 1788 and are typical of the cottages built at that time, a terrace of simple one-up and one-down dwellings. each dwelling housed a family, with communal living and sleeping, and a privy and wash-house shared between the terrace. The centre of the town moved from the old village green to the river, where the mill stood surrounded by terraces of cottages.

● Continue along Green Lane for a few more yards, until it turns right as Mill Street. Keep ahead and then turn left down a cobbled, unnamed street. This is Long Row.

Strutt, like his ex-partner Arkwright, was a benevolent if over-paternalistic employer, and the housing he provided for his workers was good by the standards of the day. As the demand for labour continued to grow,, and with it the population of the town, Strutt built more and more dwellings. Long Row dates from 1806 and the buildings on the right-hand side of the street are typical of the second wave of housing development in industrial Belper. Still in terraces, these dwellings were much more luxurious than those seen in Short Row. They were bigger, two-up and two-down, and each dwelling had its own enclosed back yard, containing its own privy and a pig-sty.

● Follow Long Row out to the main A6, and turn right.

● Cross the road at traffic lights at a road junction in front of East Mill. Go down the side road, with East Mill on your right hand, soon passing under an arch over the road.

Strutt's original mill consisted of two buildings, a North Mill and a South Mill, connected by the arch you are about to pass under. The arch enabled management to pass from one building to the other without descending to street level. Built into the arch are narrow slits, best seen on the other side: these were gun embrasures.

'Trouble at t'mill' was a real possibility in the early nineteenth century, and it was not unknown for mills to be attacked by workers disgruntled with harsh working conditions and poor wages. The employers in this part of Derbyshire were for their day enlightened and benevolent, but Strutt still thought it prudent to design his mill as a fortress able to withstand assault if necessary.

⬤ Just beyond the arch, on the right hand side, is the entrance to North Mill. *North Mill was built in 1804 by William Strutt, Jedediah's son and heir. It was built on the site of his fathers original mill, much bigger and incorporating the latest safety features. Fire was a major hazard in early factories, which contained unguarded machinery, were overcrowded, and had inadequate exits for the number of workers employed. Belper North Mill was the second oldest fireproof industrial building in the world. It was five stories high, with cast-iron columns connected by wrought-iron beams and tie rods, which in turn supported floors of hollow brick. All these features were designed to contain any fire that broke out to a small area and to stop it rushing through the building.*

North Mill continued to produce cotton yarn until 1912, when it and the adjoining South Mill were replaced by the present East Mill building.

The mill (now housing the Derwent Valley Visitor Centre) is open Thursday-Sunday 1pm-5pm. Entrance charge.

Belper Mill.

● Cross the bridge over the River Derwent.

Early factories depended upon water power for the energy to drive their machinery. Indeed, it was the fast-flowing rivers of Derbyshire that led to the area becoming the cradle of the Industrial Revolution (see walk 20). The dam on the right as you cross the bridge was built in 1797 by Jedediah Strutt to provide water for his mills. In 1819 his son William raised the dam by three foot and incorporated 12 large water wheels, the housings for which can still be seen. Over time, the river bed suffered increasing erosion due to the pressure of the water being diverted through it, and in 1843 the water course was lined with brick to prevent further erosion.

● Immediately over the bridge, turn left onto a fenced track along the river bank.

● At the end of the tarmaced track go straight on, passing a brick building on your left to go through an opening in the fence. Keep straight on along the bottom of the field on a footpath, with a wall on your left.

● Go through a squeeze stile and keep straight on, still with the wall on your left.

● Go through a squeeze stile by a gate, with an old house off to your left. Keep ahead on a broad grassy track leading back to the river bank.

● Go along the river bank for 250 yards past the old house, then turn right through a squeeze stile beside a metal field gate.

● Go half-left across a small field to a stile by a hawthorn bush.

● Continue the same line of advance up the next field, to a squeeze stile in the bushes in the top-right corner of the field.

● Keep ahead up the field along a clear track. Pass through a line of trees and continue up the field, aiming to the immediate left of a house seen on top of the slope ahead.

● Pass around the corner of a garden, with a high wall on your right, to a squeeze stile.

● Go through the stile and keep ahead down the drive to a lane.

● Turn left along the lane for 100 yards, and then, just before reaching a bungalow, turn right through a stile.

● Go straight on up the field, with a wall on your right. Cross a drive via two stiles and keep on up the field to a stile.

● Cross the stile and continue up the field to a stile at the top of the slope, leading onto a cross track.

● Turn left along the cross track. You follow this track for the next mile. Initially it is a track, that then widens into a drive, and then shrinks back to a track again. It is enclosed throughout, with views down over the Derwent Valley on your left.

- After a mile, the track shrinks to a footpath, still enclosed. A golf course is visible just ahead.

- Follow the walled path through the golf course, ignoring a footpath leading off to the right.

- The path becomes a surfaced drive. Continue straight on along the drive, ignoring a turn to the right and still with golf course fairways and greens on both sides of you.

- Pass a ventilation tower for the Milford Tunnel on your left.

The railway was built down the Derwent Valley in the mid-nineteenth century. Unlike the turnpike, which wound down the banks of the river, the railway needed to follow a course that was as straight as possible, and was unable to follow the Derwent as it twisted through a sharp and narrow gorge at Milford. Consequently, it was necessary to bore a tunnel over half a mile long and 220 feet deep through the spur of hillside you are descending.

- Descend with the drive, soon passing a house on your left. The drive becomes a tarmaced residential lane. Continue ahead down the lane, soon a steep hill.

- At a T-junction at the bottom of the hill, with a primary school facing you, go straight on across the road and down an alley to the A6. The Strutt Arms is on your right.

The names of public houses often reflect the salient features of a locality's history. The Strutt family were the major employers in this valley for a century, and controlled every aspect of the lives of their workers. The Strutt Arms, built in the early part of the nineteenth century, reflects in its name the family's pre-eminence.

- Turn left along the A6, passing Milford Mill on your left, and cross the River Derwent.

Milford Mill was built by Jedediah Strutt and Richard Arkwright in 1780. When their partnership was dissolved the following year, Strutt kept the mill at Milford as well as Belper Mill, whilst Arkwright retained the mills at Cromford.

- Immediately over the river, turn right in front of the King William IV public house, signed to 'Makeney'. Go down the road, with the river and two splendid weirs on your right.

- Pass the Riverside Garden Centre on the right, and 200 yards later, opposite The Makeney Hotel, turn left up a lane, passing the entrance to White Gables on the corner on your right.

- At the top of the rise, just before reaching the Holly Bush Inn on the right, turn left up a lane, with a Public Bridleway sign.

- Where the lane ends at a gate, with the gateway to Makeney Mews on the left, continue straight on up a bridleway ahead.

- Continue up the enclosed bridleway, muddy at times, climbing steadily.

● Swing left with the bridleway, still climbing and still enclosed, ignoring all sides turns, to emerge onto a tarmaced track beside gate posts.

● Turn left along the track.

There are views to the left over the Derwent Valley, with the ventilation tower for the railway clearly visible on the hillside opposite.

● Follow the track out to a lane. Turn left along the lane for 350 yards. Where the lane starts to descend, just after passing through a stand of trees, look out for steps set in the wall on the right.

● Climb up the steps and follow a waymarked footpath, with a wall on your right.

● Go through a squeeze stile and continue ahead along the left-hand edge of a field, with the land dropping away to the left.

● Pass through a squeeze stile and keep straight on, now with a wall on your left hand and a field on your right.

● Drop down to another squeeze stile and keep straight on along the bottom of a field, now with a wood on your left.

● At the end of the wood, keep straight on to an obvious squeeze stile 50 yards ahead. Go through the stile and turn left along a track, passing the farm on your right-hand side.

● Follow the track for nearly half a mile as it descends and then climb again to reach a road.

● Turn right along the road for 100 yards. Where the road turns sharp right, ignore a path continuing ahead but instead turn left onto a tarmaced path, with bungalows on your right.

● At the end of the bungalows keep straight on with a field on the right. Where the fence on your left ends, keep straight on across the open field. The path soon becomes enclosed and tarmaced again, with gardens on the left.

● Descend with the path. DO NOT deviate left into the recreation field but keep ahead to descend with the path through trees.

● Maintain your line of advance. Pass behind goalposts and a hedge, to pass to the immediate right of the end of a row of houses in front. Emerge onto a tarmaced path, leading up to these houses.

● Maintain your line of advance downhill, through a metal barrier and behind factory walls to emerge into New Breck Road.

● Turn left for 5 yards, then turn right up to a more major road (Queen Street).

● Follow Queen Street for 100 yards to a junction with a main road.

● Turn right uphill up this main road for 80 yards, then turn left into the shop-lined King Street, Belper's main shopping area.

- Go down King Street for 50 yards, then turn right up Green Lane, opposite a Memorial Garden and with a car park on the corner.
- Go along Green Lane, soon crossing Church Lane on your right and returning to the entrance gates to St Peter's Church on your right.

Magpie Mine: the heyday of Peakland lead mining

Distance: 5 miles

Map: OS sheet 119

Start and parking: The walk starts from the pay & display car park on the A6, two miles to the west of Ashford in the Water (grid ref: 171706). However, this car park closes at 4pm for at least periods of the year, and limited alternative parking is a lay-by one mile further east, in the direction of Ashford. This lay-by is almost en route, and directions to it are given in the text.

Refreshments: none.

Historical Background

Lead mining has been a major part of the economy of Derbyshire for more than two thousand years. The White Peak area was renowned for its lead during the Iron Age, and to gain control of this commodity was one of the reasons for the Roman occupation in 70-80AD. The Romans themselves mined and exported lead, and ingots were found throughout the Empire bearing the name 'Lutudarum' (the name of the administrative centre of the lead mining industry in Derbyshire, possibly in the vicinity of modern Wirksworth). With the arrival of the Normans there was a great increase in demand for Derbyshire lead, for the building of castles, monasteries and great houses. The Domesday Book records lead smelting sites in Bakewell, Matlock, Wirksworth, and Ashford. Lead from Derbyshire was used in Westminster Abbey and even exported: 200 tons were sent to Clairvaux Abbey in France in the twelfth century.

The heyday of lead mining in the peaks was 1700-1750, when at least 10,000 miners worked in the industry. Rich veins of lead, known as 'rakes', ran for miles through the limestone, sometimes near the surface but often as deep as 500 feet underground. The shallower rakes were dug out by open cast mining, but by the seventeenth century all the shallow rakes had been worked out. Pits of varying depths and complexity were then dug to reach the deeper deposits. Deep pit mining however would always reach the water table eventually, and the mine would be flooded. To prevent this, drainage tunnels or 'soughs' were dug, sloping from the bottom of the mine to a lower valley some distance away, down which the flood water could be drained. Lead once extracted was often smelted near to the mine. Open pits known as 'bole holes' were dug, containing a primitive hearth in which lead ore could be partially melted and moulded into saleable ingots or 'pigs'. Bole holes are often on the western flanks of hills, where they could catch the wind and thus force a draught into the hearth.

Although lead mining has ceased on the White Peak, the landscape still bears the scars, with up to 50,000 mine shafts, 30 soughs and countless bole holes still to be seen. The most complete and interesting example of lead mining in the Peak is to be found however at Magpie Mine.

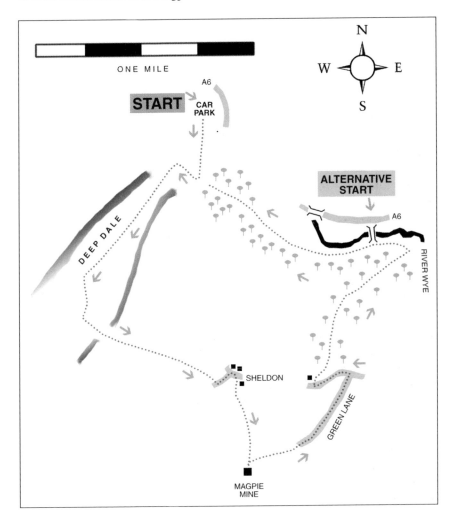

The Walk

This walk ascends the dramatic Deepdale before crossing open fields, containing many reminders of the lead mining industry, to reach Magpie Mine, one of the best preserved lead mines in England. The walk then returns through wooded valleys and along the bank of the River Wye.

● From the pay & display car park, go up the footpath at the back of the parking area, beside the ticket machine. Cross a stile and go along a surfaced path, with the A6 down on the left.

● After crossing a second stile the path is unsurfaced and soon swings away from the A6. Contour around the hillside with the path, ignoring a side turning uphill.

● Join a wall on your left and shortly cross a stile on the left.

● Follow the path through a gully and uphill.

● At a T-junction, turn right signed 'Deepdale'. Follow the clear path around the hillside.

● On meeting a wall, turn left up the valley, with the wall on your right hand.

● After one mile, when a cross wall bars your progress, go through a gate on your right.

● Continue on up the valley, with the wall now on your left.

● 60 yards later cross the wall on your left via a step stile and go straight ahead up the hillside on a distinct path.

● At the top of the slope meet the corner of a wall and keep ahead for 10 yards to a step stile in the wall ahead.

● Cross the stile and maintain your line of advance across the next field to a gate.

The fields on both side of your path have numerous disused mine shafts in them. A 'rake' of lead ran through the limestone at this point, narrow and near the surface at the Deepdale end, but getting deeper as it runs south and east, and widening to 20 foot broad. A line of pits and mines follow this rake, culminating in the Magpie Mine workings. At this end the pits are quite shallow, and are now covered with a stone cap.

● Go through the gate and maintain your line of advance along the top of the next three fields, keeping the wall on your left.

● In the fourth field, initially follow the wall on your left. Where the wall turns left, go half-left to a step stile beside a telegraph pole in the left-hand wall.

● Cross the stile and maintain your line of advance across the corner of the field to a squeeze stile 15 yards ahead.

● Keep straight on along the next field, parallel to a wall on your right, to a stile by a gate leading onto a road.

● Turn left along the road for 200 yards, then turn right along a path to a squeeze stile and footpath sign, beside a gate just to the right of a cottage.

● Go ahead along a narrow field to a step stile into a field.

● Go half-right across the field, to a step stile in the far right-hand corner.

In the centre of the field is a deep, circular depression. This is the remains of a bole hole, a primitive hearth constructed by miners to do a preliminary smelting of the lead. The open end of the hearth faces the prevailing wind, which would be funnelled under the hearth to provide a draught for the fire.

● Cross the stile and follow the wall on your left hand to a squeeze stile in the corner.

● Cross a track to a squeeze stile ahead, and then go half-right across the next two fields, aiming directly for Magpie Mine.

● Cross a final stile to enter the mine workings.

Lead was first mined here in 1739 and continued off and on for over 200 years. Mining went deeper and deeper in pursuit of the ore, and the mainshaft eventually reached a depth of 729 feet, the bottom 150 feet being below the water table. In order to reach the lower ore, numerous attempts were made to keep the bottom of the mine water-free: the stone building on the site housed a Cornish beam engine, a steam driven pump successfully developed in the Cornish tin mines and brought to the Magpie Mine in 1840. The original engine was replaced by a larger and more powerful one in 1869, but was still unable to keep the mine drained. In 1873 work commenced on a drainage tunnel or sough, running from the bottom of the mine to the River Wye, a mile-and-a-quarter to the north.

For the first 130 years that the mine was worked, miners would descend the mine by climbing down an open scaffold within the mine shaft. Once this got to be 150 deep the descent became too dangerous and a cage was installed, which was lowered and raised by a steam engine. The first engine was installed in 1869, and housed in the corrugated iron shed you can see. The winding drum still remains. As the workings got still deeper, this was replaced by an upgraded engine, steam driven and housed within a building ventilated by the square chimney you can see.

At its height Magpie Mine employed 50 miners. Lead mining was big business, and not only did mine owners make their fortunes but so too did the skilled miners, paid on a piecework basis. This led to occasional demarcation disputes. The tunnels beneath the Magpie Mine followed the North Bole Vein. The nearby Maypitt Mine worked the Great Redsoil Vein. The two veins join and in 1833 miners from the two mines met underground, both trying to extract the joined vein. Arguments about who had the rights to the ore grew increasingly acrimonious, armed sentries were placed on guard of the pit heads, and miners fought hand to hand underground. The violence culminated in Magpie miners lighting fires underground to smoke out their opponents, resulting in three Maypitt miners suffocating.

The battle to keep Magpie Mine drained eventually proved too costly to be

Magpie Mine.

worthwhile, and the Mine was finally abandoned. Today the mine workings are being restored by the Peak District Mines Historical Society.
Entry to the mine site is free.

- Retrace your steps to the step stile by which you entered the mine workings.
- Cross the stile and go half-right to a stile, just to the right of a gate.
- Go through the stile and go half-left across the corner of the field, to a conspicuous footpath sign and a stile.
- Go over the stile and keep straight on across the next field, to a stile beside a field gate leading into an enclosed green lane.
- Go down the green lane for half a mile to reach a road.
- Turn left along the road for 200 yards. Immediately before the first building on your right, turn right through a squeeze stile, and then turn sharp right to follow a path down the valley, aiming just to the right of a gate in the valley bottom.
- Pass the gate and walk with the wall on your left hand to a pedestrian gate in the bottom corner of the field.
- Keep straight ahead along the bottom of the next short field to a pedestrian gate into woods.
- Follow the path down the valley through the woods. Where the valley widens, bear right with the clear path and continue downhill through the trees.
- At the end of the woods cross a stile by a gate. Keep ahead, with the wall on your right, to reach a cross track at a wall.

- Turn left along the track, initially with the wall on your right.
- On reaching the River Wye, keep straight on across a meadow to a stile beside a gate.
- Go over the stile and keep straight on, to a disused mill beside a bridge over the river.

To start the walk at the lay-by, cross the A6 and go down a short track to a bridge over the Wye. Cross the bridge to the disused mill.

- Go behind the disused mill buildings and continue along the footpath, soon regaining the river bank.
- Follow the footpath, which stays within the edge of the woods.
- The footpath leaves the river on the opposite side of a meadow and climbs through trees to follow a bank high above the A6, soon passing over the outlet of the Magpie Mine Sough.

Magpie Mine was one of the deepest on the Peak, and the bottom 150 feet were below the water table. To drain the mine and allow the lead to be extracted a horizontal drainage tunnel or sough was dug, taking eight years to complete and being finished in 1881, at a cost of £18,000. It sloped from the bottom of the mine, and ran for one-and-a-quarter miles to discharge water from the mine into the River Wye. In 1966 the roof of the sough collapsed and its course is now just discernible as an irregular depression in the ground within the private woods to your left.

- Eventually the path crosses a wall and starts to descend. At the bottom of the slope you come to a T-junction.
- **If you started at the lay-by:** keep ahead at the T-junction, signed 'Deepdale'. The instructions for the rest of the walk are at the beginning of this chapter.
- **If you started at the car park:** turn right down a path signed 'White Lodge Picnic Area'. Follow the path down the slope and across a wall and turn right into the footpath beyond. Ignore side turns to the right but keep ahead, retracing your outward steps back to the car park.

Walk 23

Buxton: the growth of tourism

Distance: 5.5 miles

Map: OS sheet 119

Start and parking: The walk starts from the Buxton Country Park car park (entrance at grid ref: 043718). The entrance drive is on a minor road to Harpur Hill, which leads off the A54 one mile south of Buxton. The car park is signposted as caravan park and picnic area.

Refreshments: Shops, tearooms, and public houses in Buxton.

Historical Background

Buxton has been famous for its healing waters throughout its history. Mineral water trickling through the limestone for thousands of years, emerges here as thermal springs, heated to a constant 82 degrees. These waters have been reputed throughout the ages to have healing qualities for a whole range of illnesses, especially those of a rheumatic variety. To Iron Age man the grove around the spring was sacred to Arnemeta, goddess of healing. Once Britain was a settled part of the Roman Empire the garrison town they had built here, Aquae Arnemetiae, became a spa and attracted visitors from across the province. By 1460 there was a chapel here, dedicated to St Anne, and beside it a holy well, soon famous for its miraculous healing properties.

In 1535 Sir William Cavendish, appointed by Henry VIII to help oversee the Dissolution of religious houses in Derbyshire, dissolved the chapel and promptly bought the land for himself, thereby beginning the association between Buxton and the Cavendish family, after 1688 to become the Dukes of Devonshire (see walk 17).

The waters of Buxton became popular again during Elizabethan times, but it was another two hundred years before the town became a destination for visitors in any numbers. In 1778 Buxton was still a small town, with a tiny population mainly engaged in agriculture. At about this time spa towns were gaining in popularity, with fashionable Georgian society flocking to them to take, and be seen taking, the waters. The 5th Duke of Devonshire saw the commercial possibilities of exploiting Buxton's waters to create a spa to rival Bath and

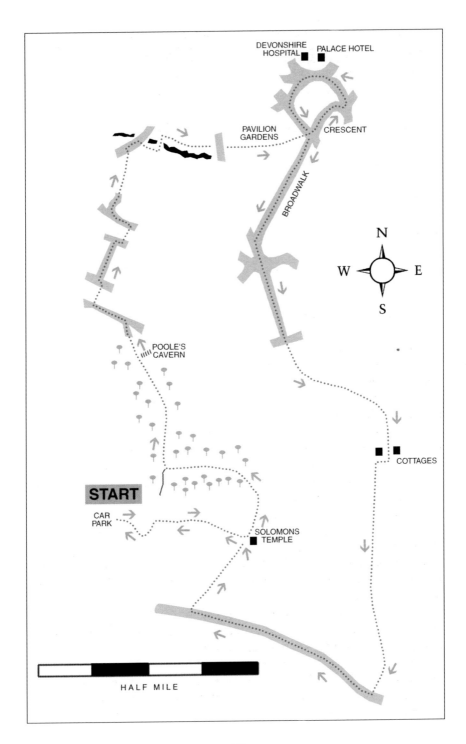

DEVONSHIRE HOSPITAL

PALACE HOTEL

PAVILION GARDENS

CRESCENT

BROADWALK

N
W   E
S

POOLE'S CAVERN

START

COTTAGES

CAR PARK

SOLOMONS TEMPLE

HALF MILE

Harrogate, and set about buying land and developing it into a spa town. Between 1780 and 1788 the core of the town was laid out around The Crescent, modelled upon the Royal Crescent in Bath and housing natural baths. St Anne's Well was re-opened, and stables and a hotel built. Buxton rapidly grew in popularity as a fashionable resort for the wealthy.

The 6th Duke was really responsible for the development of Buxton into a fully-fledged tourist town. Alive to the possibilities opened up by the arrival of the turnpike and especially the railway in 1863, he encouraged the new middle classes as well as the gentry to come and visit Buxton He greatly increased the family's holdings in the town, until by 1847, 75% of the town was owned by the Devonshire family. The Duke greatly increased the facilities of the town, building hotels, villas for the gentry, a concert hall, laying out gardens, and giving the town its first municipal hospital.

The Walk

This walk starts in Buxton County Park and visits Solomon's Temple, with fine views over Buxton. It then goes around the town itself, following the development of tourism over five centuries, before returning across fields and moor to the Park.

- With your back to the toilet block, turn left and leave the car park at the top corner, on a footpath signed 'Poole's Cavern and Solomon's Temple'.

- Climb with the footpath out of the quarry. Turn left at the top, still signed 'Solomon's Temple'.

Solomon's Temple.

● Cross a stile and make your way along an occasional path across hummocks to Solomon's Temple, clearly visible on the skyline ahead.

Solomon's Temple was built in 1896 by Solomon Mycock, a local industrialist who wanted to provide work for the local unemployed and also to leave a memorial to himself. This 25 foot tower is a lovely example of a nineteenth century folly, a mock-classical temple in the style beloved by Victorians. It is built on top of a bronze age burial mound, itself on top of a 1,440 foot hill which affords commanding views over Buxton and the surrounding countryside. The tower's official name is Grin Low Tower, but it is always known by the name of its builder.

● Leave Solomon's Temple from the door and go down the hill towards Buxton, to a squeeze stile in the wall ahead.

● Go through the stile and continue down the slope, to a gate beside a conspicuous white notice board on the edge of woods ahead.

● Cross the stile by the gate and follow the clear path into the woods.

Grin Low Woods were planted by the 5th Duke of Devonshire on land scarred by an unsightly waste tip, the by-product of centuries of quarrying and lime burning. The woods are a very early example of land reclamation, far ahead of their time. They also provided a pleasant green backdrop to the spa town the Duke was trying to create.

● Ignore side turns to left and right and follow the broad path as it descends through trees. At a T-junction, turn right, still descending.

● Follow the main track downhill, eventually passing steps, signed 'Pooles Cavern', on your right.

● Continue down the track, to join a tarmaced drive at Kabenhol Cottage. continue down the drive to a road.

● Turn left along the road for 300 yards. Pass house No.126 on your right, then turn right down a fenced footpath.

● At the end of the footpath, cross the road half-left and continue your line of advance down Hargate Road.

● At a T-junction at the end of the road, turn right for 40 yards then turn left down a footpath, just to the right of No.26.

● At the end of the footpath, turn left along the road.

50 yards down the road on the right are Milnthorp Alms Houses, built in 1904 and run as a charity to provide housing for the 'deserving poor' of Buxton.

● After 100 yards turn right down Wye Head Close.

● Follow the Close around to the right and then keep ahead along a footpath between No.23 and No.4.

● Keep straight on across a field towards trees, and then turn left to reach a road.

● Turn right along the road for 10 yards. immediately before a bridge, turn right down a tarmaced path to the side of a river. Turn right along the river.

The 6th Duke of Devonshire had employed the landscape architect Sir Joseph Paxton, later designer of London's Crystal Palace, to redesign the grounds of Chatsworth House (see walk 17), and it was natural that he should also employ Paxton for his project of beautifying Buxton. The walks you around you are called the Serpentine Walk, and employ themes Paxton used at Chatsworth and elsewhere, of flowing water snaking through trees and shrubs, themselves interspersed with hidden lawns.

● Shortly cross a footbridge and continue downstream, now with the water on your right.

● At the end of the walk go over a footbridge to reach a road. Cross the road into the park and keep straight on, with the dome of the pavilion ahead.

● Do not cross the bridge but turn right along the side of the river, keeping the water on your left-hand side.

The Pavilion was built in 1876 as a concert room by Robert Ripon Duke, using glass and iron, materials beloved by Victorian architects. It was surrounded by the Pavilion Gardens, laid out on land along the banks of the River Wye, given to the town by the 7th Duke of Devonshire. The gardens were designed by Edward Milner, who had worked with Joseph Paxton on Crystal Palace. Milner tried to imitate the effect created in the nearby Serpentine gardens by Paxton, but failed to achieve the same intimacy and delicacy with which Paxton blended trees and bushes to the contours of the land.

● Opposite the band stand and bridge to the Pavilion, keep straight ahead to leave the park to the right of buildings seen ahead (Old Hall Hotel).

Old Hall Hotel stands on the site of a Tudor building, Old Hall, built by the Earl of Shrewsbury in the sixteenth century. Shrewsbury was gaoler to Mary, Queen of Scots, during her long period of house arrest in Derbyshire. Mary suffered acutely with rheumatism and was periodically given permission to visit Buxton to take the waters. She visited the town five times between 1573 and 1584, staying each time at Shrewsbury's property, Old Hall.

On Shrewsbury's death Old Hall passed through his widow Bess of Hardwick to the Cavendish family, later Dukes of Devonshire, her descendants from her earlier marriage to Sir William Cavendish. The Old Hall was demolished and the present building put up in 1670, and as such is one of the oldest hotels in Buxton.

● Go down the side of Old Hall Hotel into the Crescent.

The Crescent is the heart of the town conceived by the 5th Duke of Devonshire. All Victorian spa towns had a parade, based upon the architecture of classical Greece, and Devonshire determined that Buxton should be no exception. He commissioned John Carr of York to build a grand crescent, modelled upon the Royal Crescent at Bath, which was duly built between 1784-88. The Crescent incorporated three hotels, an assembly room, a library and shops, as well as a building where the mineral waters of Buxton's thermal springs could be bathed in. This Natural Bath building (where the present Tourist Information Office now stands) was erected upon the site of the roman bathhouse, built for the legionnaires stationed here 2000 years previously. This crescent became the centre of fashionable Buxton.

Opposite the Crescent stands The Pump Room and beside it, St Anne's Well. This stands at the traditional heart of Buxton. A spring sacred to the goddess Arnemeta bubbled from the earth here. In the middle ages Arnemeta became the Christian Saint Anne, and waters from her spring were said to have magical healing properties, that for centuries attracted people for miles to come and visit. The Well and its associated chapel were closed during the Dissolution of the Monasteries, but re-opened in the 1570s, when the medical properties of mineral waters were enjoying a renaissance in Elizabethan society. Taking the healing waters proved so popular with people from all strata of society that an edict was soon passed, banning the poor from coming to the well without special licence. The Pump Room was built next to the well in 1894, and thermal water served to those visitors who could afford to pay for it.

● Go along the front of the Crescent and pass Cavendish Arcade on your left.
Cavendish Arcade was once the thermal baths complex, housed beneath an impressive barrel vaulted roof of stained glass. When the baths closed, the building was converted into a shopping mall, whilst preserving many of the original architectural features. Its name remembers the Cavendish family, Dukes of Devonshire.

● Turn left and follow Cavendish Arcade around. Go up the street past pedestrian lights to a traffic island.
Having decided to expand the appeal of Buxton, the 6th Devonshire needed all the

Devonshire Hospital.

179

infrastructure of a tourist town, if Buxton was to take off. The Palace Hotel (half-right, in front of you) was designed by Henry Currey (who had also built the Natural Baths building) and opened in 1867, the year that the railway first reached Buxton. Then as now it was the largest hotel in the town.

Half-left in front of you is the Devonshire Hospital, originally built in 1790 by the 5th Duke as stables for the horses of the many visitors to Buxton. 120 horses could be accommodated in the huge building. In 1857 his son and successor the 6th Duke gave part of the block and the surrounding land to the town, for use as a hospital. The magnificent dome, made of slate and with a span of 154 feet, was added in 1880 and at the time was the largest unsupported dome in the world.

● Turn left and follow the block around, to turn left down George Street.
On the left is the Pump Room for the Devonshire Hospital, where patients could take the thermal spa waters.

● Keep straight on to pass the George Hotel on your right and go along the Square.
The Square was designed by John White in 1802 as part of the complex of buildings where visitors to the Spa could stay. The building was surrounded by a roofed arcade, to allow visitors to promenade without getting wet.

Facing the square is the Opera House, the final major civic building to be added to the complex in central Buxton. It was opened in 1903, and is unashamedly Edwardian, slightly incongruous amidst the Victorian buildings around it.

Note on the right-hand corner of the Square the hexagonal pillar box dating from 1867, the only Victorian pillar box left in Derbyshire.

● At the end of the Square, turn left back to the entrance of the Old Hall Hotel. Turn right into Broadwalk, which runs along the top left-hand side of the Pavilion Gardens.
Broadwalk was designed by Joseph Paxton in the 1850s, part of the 6th Duke's expansion plan. It was to provide villa residences for the gentry visiting Buxton for the season, and also for the affluent middle classes of the town to live in all year around. The row of houses were originally named Cavendish Terrace, after the Dukes of Devonshire. When built they would have faced onto a meadow along the banks of the Wye (Pavilion Gardens were a later addition) and carriages would have been able to drive along the Broadwalk, into town and back along the riverbank.

● Keep straight on down the full length of Broadwalk to emerge at a road junction.

● Your route continues to the left of the Alison Park Hotel, whose large red sign can be seen at the far side of this complex road junction. To reach it, first cross over the road in front of you to a pillar box.

● Cross the next road, turn right and immediately turn left into College Road, following signs to 'Pooles Cavern'.

- Follow College Road to its end. Cross over and keep straight on along a path opposite.
- Keep ahead along the enclosed footpath to a gate at the end.
- Go through the gate into a field and keep straight on, with a wall on your right. Follow the wall as it curves right, to join a concrete track.
- Follow the track between cottages to a cattle grid. Immediately over the cattle grid turn right to a stile, and then turn left along the bottom of a field, with the wall on your left.
- Follow the wall over stiles along the bottom of two fields and into an enclosed footpath.
- Follow the footpath into another field. Keep ahead between farm and paddock into a track.
- Follow the track to a gate and into a field. Keep straight on up the side of the field, with a wall and trees on your left.
- Where the wall and trees end, keep straight across the open field, to a stile in the bottom left-hand corner.
- Cross the stile and keep straight on, with the wall on your left hand. Follow the wall past a gate and around to the right. At a corner, follow the wall leftwards, down to a stile on to a road.
- Turn right up the road for half a mile.
- Turn right at a footpath sign, cross a stile by a gate and go up the slope to a second stile 20 yards ahead.
- Cross the stile and keep straight on, picking your way through crags and hummocks on a vague path to Solomon's Temple, seen on the skyline ahead.
- At the Temple, turn left and descend the ridge back to the car park, aiming for the tarmac approach road ahead.

These hills and the caravan park beyond are reclaimed quarries, landscaped in 1982, and imitating the pioneering work of the Duke of Devonshire 150 years before.

Melbourne Hall and two Victorian Prime Ministers

Distance: 9.5 miles

Map: OS sheet 128

Start and parking: The walk starts from the free public car park in the centre of Ticknall (grid ref: 352240). Ticknall is on the A514 four miles north-east of Swadlincote and eight miles south of Derby. The car park is behind the community hall and clearly signposted from the main street.

Refreshments: Public houses and shop in Ticknall, public houses in Melbourne.

Historical Background

Melbourne Hall was home to two Prime Ministers of the first half of Queen Victoria's reign, men very influential in moulding the development of the monarchy as we know it today, but whose relationship with their queen was very different.

William Lamb, 2nd Viscount Melbourne, was a witty, well-informed, charming man of the world, who became Prime Minister when Earl Grey (see walk 3) resigned in 1834. Melbourne's first act was to call and to win a general election on the issue of whether the King had the right to interfere in the composition of an elected government, a milestone in delimiting the power of a constitutional monarch.

Melbourne was Prime Minister when the 18-year-old Victoria came to the throne in 1837. There was an instant rapport between the two. Victoria had little idea of the practicalities of rule, and adopted the benevolent Melbourne as a father figure (her own father had died when she was one). Melbourne, a lonely and disillusioned old man, had in turn a genuine love for his young queen. They met over dinner almost every night, and over the next four years the Prime Minister gently educated her into the duties of a constitutional monarch, the limitations on her power and the etiquette she should adopt in dealing with parliament. Victoria was distraught at losing her friend and confidante when Melbourne was forced from office in 1842.

Henry Temple, 3rd Viscount Palmerston, was a man of very different temperament, brusque and confrontational in his politics. As Foreign Secretary to Melbourne and later to Lord John Russell, he saw it his duty uphold British prestige and if necessary to encourage popular movements opposed to the autocratic rulers of Europe, if this served Britain's interests. Victoria, related to many of those autocrats Palmerston was attacking, considered that she should be actively involved in foreign affairs, and tried to use her influence to oppose his Palmerston's policies. He in consequence gave his queen as little information as possible about what he was doing, and relations between the two deteriorated steadily. Palmerston represented England at its most robust, and as such was popular in parliament and with the people, and although Victoria might fume against 'that dreadful man' she was forced to learn the salutary lesson that she was powerless to remove a minister she disliked, or to have overt control of government policy. The culmination of these lessons came in 1855, when the Queen found herself powerless to reject the will of parliament and electorate, and was forced to accept Palmerston as her Prime Minister.

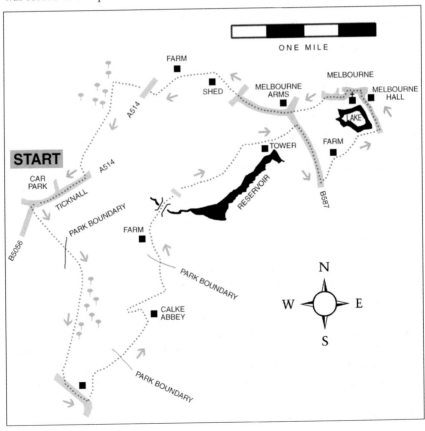

The Walk

**This walk crosses Calke Park and passes Calke Abbey before going across
country and past Staunton Harold Reservoir to visit Melbourne Hall.**

- Leave the car park and turn right to reach the main A514, opposite The Wheel
  public house.

- Turn right along the main road for 350 yards, passing a post office/stores on
  your left.

- Turn left down Ashby Road (the B5006 to Ashby). Pass The Staff of Life
  public house on your left and 50 yards later turn left at a footpath sign, by a
  mounting block.

*The mounting block is a reflection of Ticknall's rural past. The block was provided to
enabled gentlemen to mount and dismount from their horses with ease.*

- Go over a stile into a field and keep ahead up the side of the field, with a hedge
  and then a wall on your right.

- Where the wall ends, keep straight on across the field.

- Cross a stile in a gap in the hedge, and keep straight on across the next field
  to a stile, keeping the hedge off to your left.

- Cross the stile and keep straight ahead across the centre of the next field.

- Cross a stile to enter Calke Park, and turn right onto a cross track. Follow the
  path as it curves left along the top of a very slight embankment to reach a stile
  by a gate.

- Cross the stile and keep ahead down the left-hand edge of a field, with trees
  and then a wall on your left-hand side, to enter a wood.

- Follow the broad path through a band of woodland to a squeeze stile beside
  a metal field gate.

- Go through the stile and maintain your line of advance along the left-hand
  edge of a field, keeping woodland on your left-hand.

- Cross a stile and keep ahead in the next field, still with woods on your left.

- In the bottom left-hand corner of the field, go through a squeeze stile on the
  left, beside a metal field gate. Immediately turn right and maintain same line
  of advance, now with the hedge on your right.

- As you cross the field, veer away from the right-hand boundary, to pass beside
  a telegraph pole. Now maintain this line of advance to a clear stile in the
  middle of the hedge at the bottom of the field.

- Cross the stile into a lane and turn left.

- Follow the lane for 500 yards, passing a farm on the left. Where the lane turns
  sharp right, turn left onto an unmade track.

Calke Abbey.

- Follow the track along the boundary of two large fields, to a gate giving entry into Calke Park.

- Go through the gate and keep straight on along a metalled drive to reach Calke Abbey.

Nothing remains of the original Augustinian Abbey, built around the twelfth century and victim to the Dissolution of the Monasteries in 1536-39. In 1534 Henry VIII, after several years wrangling with the Pope over his desire to divorce his Queen, Katherine of Aragon, finally lost patience and passed the Act of Supremacy, making himself head of the church in England. The Pope retaliated by excommunicating King Henry, and the break with the Church of Rome was complete. Although Henry's motivation had been political, it gave the opportunity for a radical overhaul of the church. The religious orders in England owned considerable amounts of land and were to a great degree independent of the laws of the land. Corruption did exist and although its extent has been overstated, reform was long overdue.

Thomas Cromwell appointed commissioners, often local men, to review the effectiveness of the church in their own counties and recommend which religious orders and properties needed to be reduced or closed altogether. The door was obviously open for corruption and abuse. One of the commissioners for Derbyshire was Sir William Cavendish (see walks 15 and 17) who recommended the closure of most of the monasteries and abbeys in the county and who profited greatly from his own recommendations, buying land cheaply for himself or accepting huge bribes from others in return for access to church lands. The lands attached to Calke Abbey were sold off to local landowners, and the Abbey itself, after having been stripped of all its lead and other valuable building commodities, allowed to crumble into ruin.

The present Calke Abbey was built as a baroque mansion for Sir John Harpur between 1701-03 (see walk 18). The stones of the original ruin were used in the new house. The fashion of the time, displayed most noticeably at nearby Chatsworth House (see walk 17) were to surround houses with landscaped grounds, and Calke duly acquired its park, as well as a walled garden, and an orangery, recently restored. The interior of the Abbey is little changed since the eighteenth century.

Open March-November, Saturday-Wednesday, 1.00-5.30pm (gardens 11.00-5.30pm). Entrance charge, free to National Trust Members.

Beyond the Abbey is Staunton Harold Reservoir, created this century to provide drinking water to the increasingly urbanised county. Beneath its waters was Furnace Farm, so called because it was the site of a forge owned by the Melbourne Ironworks in the eighteenth century. The forge burnt charcoal created from the local forest, and turned cast iron into wrought iron.

- Turn left with the drive, passing an ex-stable block on your right hand, to reach a car park.

- Enter the car park and go along the left wall for 10 yards to reach a gate.

- Go through the gate and immediately turn right. Walk along with the wall on your right, ignoring a gate on the right at the end of the wall. Keep ahead, now with a fence on your right.

- On reaching a stile in the fence on the right, at the top of a drop, turn left along the top of the bank for 15 yards, then turn right down steps towards the ornamental pond below.

- At the foot of the steps go through a kissing-gate and follow a path along the waters edge, with the pond on your left and soon a deer fence on your right.

- Turn left with the path and deer fence to a gate on a causeway across the end of the water.

- Go through the gate and continue up the path, keeping the deer fence on your right-hand side.

- At the top of the ridge, turn left onto a cross track. In 30 yards turn right through a pedestrian gate.

- Turn left for 10 yards to a stile into a field.

- The right of way goes half-right across the field, just to the right of a farm seen ahead.

- As you cross the field, aim about 100 yards to the right of the farm, to cross a stile leading onto a farm track.

- Cross the track to another stile. Cross this and keep straight on across the next field, son to meet the left-hand boundary.

- Continue ahead along the field boundary, with a wall on your left. Ten yards BEFORE the wall curves to the left around a large single tree, and 20 yards before the end of the field, turn sharp right onto a path going across the field and downhill.

- Follow the path down to a footbridge.
- Cross the footbridge and go half-right up the field, to a gate in the top right-hand corner.
- Cross a stile beside the gate, and cross the lane to cross a stile opposite. Go half-right across the next field, to a squeeze stile beside a gate, some 100 yards to the left of the bottom corner.
- Maintain your line of advance across the corner of the next field, to a stile just to the right of a tree.
- Cross the stile and go along the bottom of a small field, with the hedge on your right hand, to exit via a stile.
- Follow the enclosed footpath to another stile, and then continue along the bottom of the next field, still with the hedge on your right hand.
- When the hedge ends, go quarter right across the field to a stile in the corner.
- Keep straight on along the top of the next three fields, with a hedge and soon telegraph wires on your left hand, and the reservoir down to your right.
- At the end of the third field, cross a stile. Keep straight on, still with the hedge and telegraph wires on your left.
- Where the hedge ends, keep ahead and follow the telegraph poles across the field, aiming towards a disused windmill.
- Go through a squeeze stile to reach the base of the tower.

The tower is all that remains of a windmill, built in 1798 by Lord Melbourne, father of the future Prime Minister and owner of all the land around. This was a 'tower windmill', with the base fixed and the sails set into a cone on the top. The cone could be revolved through 360 degrees, and was thus able to capture winds from any direction. The windmill was used for the milling of corn on his lordship's estates, and was in use until the end of the nineteenth century.

- Pass the tower on your right hand and drop Down through a picnic area to reach a gate across the access road.
- Go through the gate and bear right down the road, leaving houses up on the left and ignoring a gate on your right. Follow the road as it curves left, passes between gateposts and leads out to a road.

The Melbourne Arms is 100 yards up the road to the left. It derives its name not from the nearby town but from Lord Melbourne, who owned most of the land hereabouts and controlled not only the local economy but also owned the voters of the town, before the electoral system was reformed in the 1832 Reform Act (see walk 3). As such the Melbourne Family effectively controlled this part of Derbyshire, and their presence is reflected in the names of some of the inns that stood within their domain.

- Turn right and go down the road for 700 yards, passing Woodhouse Farm Nurseries and climbing with the road.

- Where the road bends right, turn left at a footpath post into the drive of Pool Farm. Go down the drive towards the farm.

- Immediately before the farm gate, turn right through a pedestrian gate. Pass farm buildings on your left to enter a field.

- Go half-left across the large field, to a stile in the bottom left-hand corner.

- Go through the stile and turn left down the edge of the field, to cross another stile onto the shore of the lake.

- Turn right and walk along the lake shore.

There is a fine view across the lake to the Church and Hall. There has been a church here since Norman times and the nearby hall was originally the rectory. In front is a lake, artificially extended to create a millpond.

The town of Melbourne takes its name from the 'bourne' or seasonally flowing stream, that runs through the village and feeds this lake. The Lamb family adopted the title Lord Melbourne from the name of the village which housed their family home, and the Australian city was named after the English Prime Minister, William Lamb, Lord Melbourne.

- At the shore end turn left along a road, still with the lake on your left.

The walls of the grounds of Melbourne Hall are on your right, and shortly you pass an old mill, now converted into a private home, on your left. In the middle ages building a mill required a licence, and this was a feudal gift granted either directly by the King or delegated to his local baron. The acquisition of a mill gave considerable economic power to its owner, since he had the monopoly upon the grinding of locally produced cereal into flour, an essential commodity in rural life, and could command a percentage of the value of everything produced. Thus the licence to build a mill was a valuable commodity, and the number of mills were restricted to maintain their monopoly.

- At the end of the lake follow the road out to a main road, passing between the hall and the church.

The present church of St Michael & St Mary dates from 1150, and was built by the Bishops of Carlisle, who as well as caring for Derbyshire's spiritual life were major landowners in the county, and who owned the manor of Melbourne. They extended an existing Saxon church and built lavishly in a Romanesque style imported from Germany, much of which remains unaltered. The tower was heightened in 1602 and the western towers added in Victorian times, but the body of the church is still splendidly Norman. The Bishops of Carlisle built a tithebarn, (still standing), in front of the church, to house the agricultural produce of the neighbourhood which they collected in rent. They also built a home for the rector in 1280, which was subsequently converted into Melbourne Hall.

Melbourne Hall and Church.

Sir John Coke (pronounced Cook), Secretary of State to Charles I, acquired Melbourne Rectory from the Bishop of Carlisle in 1628, intending to convert it into a comfortable county mansion for his retirement. In the event the Civil War intervened, and most of the conversion was left to his great-grandson Thomas, vice-chamberlain to Queen Anne. The rear of the house and the north front are left over from the original mediaeval rectory, whilst the east façade is in the Queen Anne style.

Ownership of the Hall passed to Peniston Lamb, who was elevated to the peerage in 1770 and took the title of Lord Melbourne. His son William was born here and spend most of his youth in the Hall. As an adult with aspirations to a political career William spend much of his time in London, but returned to the tranquillity of Melbourne Hall at intervals. He came here to lick his wounds and let the scandal die down after his wife Lady Caroline ran off with Lord Byron, an emotional blow which scarred William, by then 2nd Lord Melbourne, for the rest of his life. After being defeated as Prime Minister in 1842, Melbourne retired to the Hall, from where he continued to correspond regularly if unconstitutionally with his friend Queen Victoria.

William died without issue and the Hall passed to his sister Emily, the widowed Lady Cowper (pronounced Cooper) who remarried to Lord Palmerston, by then Prime Minister. Like Melbourne before him, Palmerston used the Hall as a tranquil retreat from the rigours of political life in London. Palmerston was active in the social life of the county, and during one of his sojourns here was canvassed by his neighbour Florence Nightingale to support her reforms of the Army Medical System (see walk 14). **Melbourne Hall is open to the public daily except Mondays throughout August, 2pm-5pm. Admission charge.**

- Turn left along the main road for 100 yards, opposite the Blue Bell Inn, turn left into Penn Lane.

- Follow Penn Lane as it winds and climbs. Where Salisbury Lane joins from the right, keep straight on, passing a chapel school on your left.

The school was established in 1822 to provide education for local boys up to the age of 14, a considerably enlightened act, for at that time universal state education did not exist, but relied upon the charitable works, mainly of religious orders. Education for girls was not considered necessary, and the first girls school came much later.

- 200 yards past the school, turn left at a footpath post, signed 'Woodhouses'.

- Follow the footpath for a 150 yards, past a stand of trees. Just past the trees, DO NOT follow the path ahead and downhill, but turn right with the hedge on your right and follow the hedge to a wooden barrier.

- Go through the barrier and keep straight on, initially with the hedge on your right, to a stile in front of houses.

- Turn left along the road for 50 yards. Just past the Melbourne Arms, turn right up Robinsons Hill.

- Follow Robinsons Hill for half a mile, to a T-junction with Cockshut Lane/The Common. Go straight on up an unmade track opposite (Riding Bank).

- At the end of the track pass a shed (used as an industrial unit) on your left and keep straight on along the right-hand side of a large field.

- At the end of the field, go through a pedestrian gate beside a field gate, and then go half-left up the next field, aiming for the farm seen ahead.

- 10 yards short of the top left-hand corner of the field, go through a gate in the left-hand hedge. Maintain your line of advance up the next field, with the hedge on your right, to a gate.

- Go through the gate and cross the track to pass through the gate opposite.

- Go up the field, keeping the hedge on your left. Follow the field boundary as it bends right to a gate onto the A514.

- Cross the road and keep ahead up the bridleway opposite.

There are fine open views from this field, across the valley of the Trent to Derby beyond. The newly-created National Forest Authority is currently looking at much of the land in this area, reviewing each farm as it comes up for sale with a view to purchasing it to become part of the National Forest. This is a huge project to reinstate much of the old Sherwood Forest that used to cover this land. Natural broadleaf deciduous trees such as oak, ash and cherry are being planted, interspersed with commercial plantations of larch and arboretums of special interest trees.

- At the edge of woodland, go through a gate and immediately turn left along a path, just inside the wood.

- Follow the path, keeping a field on your left hand. Where the path turns sharp right, keep straight on for 10 yards, field still on your left, to emerge into an open field.
- Keep straight on across the field. On the far side, cross a track to a stile opposite.
- Cross the stile and keep straight on down the next field, with the hedge on your left.
- Cross a stile at the end of the field and keep straight on, still with hedge on your left.
- Go through a farm gate and then go half-right down the next field to a metal field gate.
- Go through a wooden gate to the left of the field gate and keep straight on across a green to the road.

To your left an arch crosses the road. This carried the Ticknall Tramway, an ancestor of modern railways along which wagons were drawn by horses. Unlike modern railways, the wagons themselves had unflanged wheels and instead, the rails were flanged. The tramway was designed by Benjamin Outram, who also worked upon the Cromford Canal (see walk 20), to take lime quarried at Ticknall to the Ashby-de-la-Zouch Canal and thence to a nation-wide market. Ticknall Tramway was opened in 1803 and operated until 1913, the years of Ticknall's industrial boom. Today the village has reverted to a largely agricultural economy.

- Turn right along the road for 200 yards. Turn right opposite The Wheel public house and go up the road back to the car park.